CAMBRIDGE LIBRARY COLLECTION

Books of enduring scholarly value

Travel and Exploration

The history of travel writing dates back to the Bible, Caesar, the Vikings and the Crusaders, and its many themes include war, trade, science and recreation. Explorers from Columbus to Cook charted lands not previously visited by Western travellers, and were followed by merchants, missionaries, and colonists, who wrote accounts of their experiences. The development of steam power in the nineteenth century provided opportunities for increasing numbers of 'ordinary' people to travel further, more economically, and more safely, and resulted in great enthusiasm for travel writing among the reading public. Works included in this series range from first-hand descriptions of previously unrecorded places, to literary accounts of the strange habits of foreigners, to examples of the burgeoning numbers of guidebooks produced to satisfy the needs of a new kind of traveller - the tourist.

The Instructions to be Prepared for the Scientific Expedition to the Antarctic Regions

The 1839–43 Antarctic expedition was primarily a scientific voyage. James Clark Ross, a member of the expedition that had located the Magnetic North Pole in 1831, was the natural choice to lead this mission to find the Magnetic South Pole. Although he was unsuccessful in this aim, he charted the coastline of most of the continent, collected valuable scientific data and made several important discoveries. Published in 1840, these papers were prepared by the Royal Society for the expedition and give detailed instructions on how to make the important magnetic and meteorological observations. There are further instructions, such as how to preserve animal specimens, and surprisingly a request to investigate the reasons for the poor cultivation of vines at the Cape of Good Hope as 'the bad quality of Cape wine ... is well known'. These papers reveal the expectations and demands placed upon this expedition.

Cambridge University Press has long been a pioneer in the reissuing of out-of-print titles from its own backlist, producing digital reprints of books that are still sought after by scholars and students but could not be reprinted economically using traditional technology. The Cambridge Library Collection extends this activity to a wider range of books which are still of importance to researchers and professionals, either for the source material they contain, or as landmarks in the history of their academic discipline.

Drawing from the world-renowned collections in the Cambridge University Library and other partner libraries, and guided by the advice of experts in each subject area, Cambridge University Press is using state-of-the-art scanning machines in its own Printing House to capture the content of each book selected for inclusion. The files are processed to give a consistently clear, crisp image, and the books finished to the high quality standard for which the Press is recognised around the world. The latest print-on-demand technology ensures that the books will remain available indefinitely, and that orders for single or multiple copies can quickly be supplied.

The Cambridge Library Collection brings back to life books of enduring scholarly value (including out-of-copyright works originally issued by other publishers) across a wide range of disciplines in the humanities and social sciences and in science and technology.

The Instructions to be Prepared for the Scientific Expedition to the Antarctic Regions

THE ROYAL SOCIETY

CAMBRIDGE
UNIVERSITY PRESS

CAMBRIDGE UNIVERSITY PRESS

Cambridge, New York, Melbourne, Madrid, Cape Town,
Singapore, São Paolo, Delhi, Mexico City

Published in the United States of America by Cambridge University Press, New York

www.cambridge.org
Information on this title: www.cambridge.org/9781108050135

© in this compilation Cambridge University Press 2012

This edition first published 1840
This digitally printed version 2012

ISBN 978-1-108-05013-5 Paperback

REPORT

OF

THE PRESIDENT AND COUNCIL

OF

THE ROYAL SOCIETY

ON THE INSTRUCTIONS TO BE PREPARED

FOR

THE SCIENTIFIC EXPEDITION

TO

THE ANTARCTIC REGIONS.

———————

LONDON:

PRINTED BY RICHARD AND JOHN E. TAYLOR,
RED LION COURT, FLEET STREET.

1840.

CONTENTS.

REPORT,

&c.

THE PRESIDENT AND COUNCIL OF THE ROYAL SOCIETY
having recommended to Her Majesty's Government
the equipment of an Antarctic Expedition for scientific
objects, were informed by the Lords Commissioners
of the Admiralty that it had been determined to send
out Captain James Clark Ross on such an expedition,
and the Council were at the same time requested to
communicate to them, for their information, any suggestions on those subjects, or on other points to which
they might wish Captain Ross's attention to be called,
in preparing the instructions to that officer*. The
Council, having due regard to the magnitude and importance of the question submitted to them, considered
that they would best fulfil the wishes of Her Majesty's
Government, by a subdivision of the inquiry into different parts, and by referring the separate consideration of each part to distinct Committees, consisting of
those members of the Society who were especially
conversant with the particular branches of science to
which each division of the inquiry had relation. These
several Committees, namely, those of Physics, of Meteorology, of Geology and Mineralogy, of Botany and
Vegetable Physiology, and of Zoology and Animal
Physiology, after bestowing much time and great attention in the investigation of the subjects brought
under their notice, have each drawn up very full and

---

* This request was conveyed in a letter from Sir John Barrow, addressed to
the Secretary of the Royal Society, and dated June 13, 1839.

complete Reports of the results of their labours. These reports have been considered and adopted by the Council, and have been incorporated in the following General Report, which the Council present as their opinion on the matters which have been referred to them by Her Majesty's Government. They take this opportunity of declaring their satisfaction at the prospect of the benefits which are likely to accrue to science from the expedition thus liberally undertaken by the Government on the representations made to them by the Royal Society and other scientific bodies in this country, and in conformity with a wise and enlightened policy. They also desire to express their grateful sense of the prompt attention which has been uniformly paid to their suggestions, and of the ample provision which has been made for the accomplishment of the various objects of the expedition.

Royal Society, 8th August, 1839.

Section I.—PHYSICS AND METEOROLOGY.

The Council of the Royal Society are very strongly impressed with the number and importance of the desiderata in physical and meteorological science, which may wholly or in part be supplied by observations made under such highly favourable and encouraging circumstances as those afforded by the liberality of Her Majesty's Government on this and other occasions, or which may be expected from the zeal and industry of travellers, residents in foreign countries, and others whose position may give them favourable opportunities of stimulating research on the part of those in their respective departments. While they wish therefore to omit nothing in their enumeration of those objects which appear to them deserving of attentive inquiry on sound scientific grounds, and from which consequences may be drawn of real importance, either for the settlement of disputed questions, or for the advancement of knowledge in any of its branches,—they deem it equally their duty to omit or pass lightly over several points which, although not without a certain degree of interest, may yet be regarded in the present state of science rather as matters of abstract curiosity than as affording data for strict reasoning; as well as others, which may be equally well or better elucidated by inquiries instituted at home and at leisure.

1. Terrestrial Magnetism.

The subject of most importance, beyond all question, to which the attention of Captain James Clark Ross and his officers can be turned, —and that which must be considered as, in an emphatic manner, the great scientific object of the Expedition,—is that of Terrestrial Magnetism; and this will be considered: 1st, as gards those accessions to our knowledge which may be supplied by observations to be made during the progress of the Expedition, independently of any concert with or co-operation of other observers; and 2ndly, as regards those which depend on and require such concert; and are therefore to be considered with reference to the observations about to be carried on simultaneously in the fixed magnetic observatories established by Her Majesty's Government, and in the other similar observatories, both public and private, in Europe, India, and elsewhere, with which it is intended to open and maintain a correspondence.

Now it may be observed, that these two classes of observations naturally refer themselves to two chief branches into which the

B

science of terrestrial magnetism in its present state subdivides itself, and which bear a certain analogy to the theories of the elliptic movements of the planets, and of their periodical and secular perturbations. The first comprehends the actual distribution of the magnetic influence over the globe, at the present epoch, in its mean or average state, when the effects of temporary fluctuations are either neglected, or eliminated by extending the observations over a sufficient time to neutralize their effects. The other comprises the history of all that is not permanent in the phenomena, whether it appear in the form of momentary, daily, monthly, or annual change and restoration, or in progressive changes not compensated by counter changes, but going on continually accumulating in one direction, so as in the course of many years to alter the mean amount of the quantities observed. These last-mentioned changes hold the same place, in the analogy above alluded to, with respect to the mean quantities and temporary fluctuations, that the secular variations in the planetary movements must be regarded as holding, with respect to their mean orbits on the one hand, and their perturbations of brief period on the other.

There is, however, this difference, that in the planetary theory all these varieties of effect have been satisfactorily traced up to a single cause, whereas in that of terrestrial magnetism this is so far from being demonstrably the case, that the contrary is not destitute of considerable probability. In fact, the great features of the magnetic curves, and their general displacements and changes of form over the whole surface of the earth, would seem to be the result of causes acting in the interior of the earth, and pervading its whole mass; while the annual and diurnal variations of the needle, with their train of subordinate periodical movements, may, and very probably do arise from, and correspond to electric currents produced by periodical variations of temperature at its surface, due to the sun's position above the horizon, or in the ecliptic, modified by local causes; while local or temporary electric discharges, due to thermic, chemical, or mechanical causes, acting in the higher regions of the atmosphere, and relieving themselves irregularly or at intervals, may serve to render account of those unceasing, and as they seem to us casual movements, which recent observations have placed in so conspicuous and interesting a light. The electrodynamic theory, which refers all magnetism to electric currents, is silent as to the causes of those currents, which may be various, and which only the analysis of their effects can teach us to regard as internal, superficial, or atmospheric.

It is not merely for the use of the navigator that charts, giving a general view of the lines of Magnetic Declination, Inclination, and Intensity, are necessary. Such charts, could they really be depended on, and were they in any degree complete, would be of the most eminent use to the theoretical inquirer, not only as general directions in the choice of empirical formulæ, but as powerful instruments for facilitating numerical investigation, by the choice they afford of data favourably arranged; and above all, as affording decidedly the best means of comparing any given theory with observation. In fact, upon the whole, the readiest, and beyond comparison the fairest and most effectual mode of testing the numerical applicability of a theory of terrestrial magnetism, would be, not servilely to calculate its results for given localities, however numerous, and thereby load its apparent errors with the real errors, both of observation and of local magnetism; but to compare the totality of the lines in our charts with the corresponding lines, as they result from the formulæ to be tested, when their general agreement or disagreement will not only show how far the latter truly represent the facts, but will furnish distinct indications of the modifications they require.

Unfortunately for the progress of our theories, however, we are yet very far from possessing charts even of that one element, the Declination, most useful to the navigator, which satisfy these requisites; while as respects the others (the Inclination and Intensity the most lamentable deficiencies occur, especially in the Antarctic regions. To make good these deficiencies by the continual practice of every mode of observation appropriate to the circumstances in which the observer is placed throughout the voyage, will be one of the great objects to which attention must be directed. And first—

At sea.—We are not to expect from magnetic observations made at sea the precision of which they are susceptible on land. Nevertheless, it has been ascertained that not only the Declination, but the Inclination and Intensity can be observed, in moderate circumstances of weather and sea, with sufficient correctness, to afford most useful and valuable information, if patience be bestowed, and proper precautions adopted. The total intensity, it is ascertained, can be measured with some considerable degree of certainty by the adoption of a statical method of observation recently devised by Mr. Fox, whose instrument will be a part of the apparatus provided. And when it is recollected that but for such observations the whole of that portion of the globe which is covered by the ocean must remain for ever a blank in our charts, it will be needless further to insist on the necessity of making a daily series of magnetic observations, in all the three particulars abovementioned, whenever weather and sea will permit, an essential feature in the business of the voyage, in both ships. Magnetic observations at sea will, of course, be affected by the ship's magnetism, and this must be eliminated to obtain results of any service. To this end,

First. Every series of observations made on board should be accompanied with a notice of the direction by compass of the ship's head at the time.

Secondly. Previous to sailing, a very careful series of the apparent deviations, as shown by two compasses permanently fixed, (the one as usual, the other in a convenient position, considerably more forward in the ship,) in every position of the ship's head, as compared with the real position of the ship, should be made and recorded, with a view to attempt procuring the constants of the ship's action according to M. Poisson's theory*; and this process should be repeated on one or more convenient occasions during the voyage; and, generally, while at anchor, every opportunity should be taken of swinging round the ship's head to the four cardinal points, and executing in each position a complete series of the usual observations.

Thirdly. Wherever magnetic instruments are landed and observations made on *terra firma*, or on ice, the opportunity should be

* Note on M. Poisson's theory of the deviation produced in the direction of the compass by the iron of the ship.

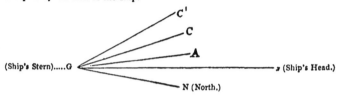

Let G x be the axis of the ship, x lying towards the ship's head.

G the centre of gravity of the compass.

G N the meridian, N the north.

Let A be the *south pole* of the dipping needle, that is the extremity of the needle which dips *beneath* the horizontal plane in our hemisphere, let C be the projection of the point A upon a horizontal plane, so that G C is the magnetic meridian. Let the angle A G C = θ, θ varying from $-90°$ to $+90°$, being positive when the south pole A is *beneath* the horizontal plane, and negative in the contrary case.

Let C G N = ψ, this angle (*variation*) which is the azimuth of the vertical plane C G A may extend from $-180°$ to $+180°$, and is to be considered *positive* or *negative* according as the line G C falls to the *west* or to the *east* of the line G N, or this angle may be considered to vary from 0 to 360°, going from north to south through *west* and returning from south to north by *east*.

Let G C' be the direction of a horizontal needle, so that C'G C is the *local attraction*.

Let x G C' = ζ $\qquad$ C'G C = δ $\qquad$ x G C = $\zeta - \delta$.
$\quad$ N G C' = ψ' $\qquad$ $\delta = \psi' - \psi$.

Let ω be the azimuth of the principal section of the ship reckoned from G N towards the *west*,

$\quad$ x G N = ω $\qquad$ $\psi' - \omega = \zeta$ $\qquad$ $\psi - \omega = \zeta - \delta$

M. Poisson arrives at the following equation, *Conn. de Temps*, 1841, p. 146, and *Mem. de l'Institut*, tom. xvi. p. 529.

$$\left.\begin{array}{l} [A' \cos \theta \cos (\psi - \omega) + B \cos \theta \sin (\psi - \omega) + C \sin \theta] \sin \zeta \\ \quad = [D \cos \theta \cos (\psi - \omega) + E' \cos \theta \sin (\psi - \omega) + F \sin \theta] \cos \zeta \end{array}\right\} \quad (1.)$$

A', B, C, D, E', F are constants, if therefore

$$\frac{B}{A'} = c, \ \frac{C}{A'} = a, \ \frac{D}{A'} = d, \ \frac{E'}{A} = b, \text{ and } \frac{F}{A'} = e$$

$\cos (\zeta - \delta) \sin \zeta + c \sin (\zeta - \delta) \sin \zeta + a \tan \theta \cos \zeta,$

$\quad = d \cos (\zeta - \delta) \cos \zeta + b \sin (\zeta - \delta) \cos \zeta + e \tan \theta \cos \zeta.$

in which equation a, b, c, d, e are constants, which must be determined from observations at some one place, and which continue invariable as long as the position of the iron in the ship remains unaltered. In order to do this the local attractions corresponding to every azimuth of the ship's head must be obtained and may be inserted in a table, or at least they must be found in sufficient number to afford any others by interpolation. The manner of obtaining such data from ob-

seized of going through the regular series on ship-board with more than usual diligence and care, so as to establish by actual experiment in the only unexceptionable manner the nature and amount of the corrections due to the ship's action for that particular geographical position, and by the assemblage of all such observations to afford data for concluding them in general.

Fourthly. No change possible to be avoided should be made in the

---

servation is described in the small code of instructions which accompanies Mr. Barlow's plate, and is also given in the Nautical Magazine.

$\psi =$ $\theta =$

Direction of ship's head. $\omega.$ x G N.	Local attraction. $\delta.$ C' G C.	Observed. $\zeta.$ x G C'.	$\zeta - \delta.$ x G C.

N.B. *This Table to be filled up from observation.*

If $\zeta = 0$,

$$- \sin \delta_1 = \frac{d \cos \delta_1 + e \tan \theta}{b}$$

if $\zeta = 180°$

$$- \sin \delta_2 = \frac{- d \cos \delta_2 + e \tan \theta}{b}$$

if $\zeta = 90°$

$$- \sin \delta_3 = c \cos \delta_3 + a \tan \delta$$

if $\zeta = 270°$

$$\sin \delta_4 = - c \cos \delta_4 + a \tan \theta$$

from these four equations, if $d = m b, e = n b, a, c, m$ and n may easily be found, and b may be then obtained from any other known deviation.

By solving equation (1.) with respect to $\tan \zeta$, the angle ζ may be found corresponding to the angle $\zeta - \delta$,

$$\tan \zeta = \frac{d \cos (\zeta - \delta) + b \sin (\zeta - \delta) + e \tan \theta}{\cos (\zeta - \delta) + c \sin (\zeta - \delta) + a \tan \theta}.$$

Afterwards, by interpolation or reversion, the angle $\zeta - \delta$ may be obtained corresponding to the *observed angle* ζ, and a table of double entry formed, giving the *local attraction* for every value of ζ, the *arguments* of the table being the *observed angle* ζ and the *dip*. This table, according to the theory of M. Poisson, ought to continue available in all quarters of the globe so long as the disposition of the masses of iron in the ship remains unaltered.

If when the ship's head is on the magnetic north and south, no effects arise from local attraction, as was the case in the experiments of Captain Flinders, $\delta_1 = 0$, $\delta_2 = 0$, and hence $d = 0, e = 0$.

If the iron is symmetrically situate about the axis of the ship, then according to M. Poisson $c = 0, d = 0, e = 0$.

disposition of considerable masses of iron in the ships during the whole voyage; but if such change be necessary, it should be noted.

Fifthly. When crossing the magnetic line of no dip it would be desirable to go through the observation for the dip with the instrument successively placed in a series of different magnetic azimuths, by which the influence of the ship's magnetism in a vertical direction will be placed in evidence.

On land, or on ice.—As the completeness and excellence of the instruments with which the Expedition will be furnished will authorise the utmost confidence in the results obtained by Captain Ross's well-known scrupulosity and exactness in their use, the redetermination of the magnetic elements at points where they are already considered as ascertained, will be scarcely less desirable than their original determination at stations where they have never before been observed. This is the more to be insisted on, as lapse of time changes these elements in some cases with considerable rapidity; and it is therefore of great consequence that observations to be compared should be as nearly cotemporary as possible, and that data should be obtained for eliminating the effects of secular variations during short intervals of time, so as to enable us to reduce the observations of a series to a common epoch.

On the other hand it cannot be too strongly recommended, studiously to seek every opportunity of landing on points (magnetically speaking) unknown, and determining the elements of those points

---

$$\cos(\zeta - \delta)\sin\zeta + a\tan\theta\sin\zeta = b\sin(\zeta - \delta)\cos\zeta. \quad . \quad . \quad (2.)$$

Conn. de Temps, p. 150.

$$\tan\zeta = \frac{b\sin(\zeta - \delta)}{\cos(\zeta - \delta) + a\tan\theta}.$$

$$\sin\delta = \frac{\sin\zeta\left\{(b-1)\cos\zeta - a\tan\theta\right\}}{1 + (b-1)\cos^2\zeta} \quad \text{nearly.}$$

If δ' is the *local attraction*, ζ' the magnetic bearing of any compass in any other distant part of the ship, or of the same compass after the disposition of the iron has been changed,

$$\cos(\zeta' - \delta')\sin\zeta' + a'\tan\theta\sin\zeta' = b'\sin(\zeta' - \delta')\cos\zeta'$$

but $\zeta' - \delta' = \zeta - \delta$

hence $\cos(\zeta - \delta)\sin\zeta + a'\tan\theta\sin\zeta' = b'\sin(\zeta - \delta)\cos\zeta'$

eliminating $\tan\theta$

$$\tan(\zeta - \delta) = \frac{(a' - a)\sin\zeta'\sin\zeta}{a'b\sin\zeta'\cos\zeta - ab'\sin\zeta\cos\zeta'}.$$

From this equation it may be possible to compute a table of double entry, giving the local attraction without knowing the dip, the arguments of the table being the *observed angles* ζ of two compasses situate in different parts of the vessel. This table ought to continue available so long as the disposition of the masses of iron remains unaltered. The two compasses must of course be so distant as to have no sensible effect upon each other.

The theory of Mr. Barlow's plate, according to M. Poisson, depends upon the practicability of so disposing the iron in the vessel as to give to the constants a and b in equation (2.) the particular values $a = 0$, $b = 1$.

with all possible precision. Nor should it be neglected, whenever the slightest room for doubt subsists, to determine at the same time the geographical position of the stations of observation in latitude and longitude. When the observations are made on ice, it is needless to remark that this will be universally necessary.

With this general recommendation it will be unnecessary to enumerate particular localities. In fact, it is impossible to accumulate too many. Nor can it be doubted that in the course of antarctic exploration, many hitherto undiscovered points of land will be encountered, each of which will, of course, become available as a magnetic station, according to its accessibility and convenience.

There are certain points in the regions about to be traversed in this voyage which offer great and especial interest in a magnetic point of view. These are, first, the south magnetic pole (or poles), intending thereby the point or points in which the horizontal intensity vanishes and the needle tends vertically downwards; and secondly, the points of maximum intensity, which, to prevent the confusion arising from a double use of the word poles, we may provisionally term magnetic *foci*.

It is not to be supposed that Captain Ross, having already signalized himself by attaining the northern magnetic pole, should require any exhortation to induce him to use his endeavours to reach the southern. On the contrary, it might better become us to suggest for his consideration, that no scientific datum of this description, nor any attempt to attain very high southern latitudes, can be deemed important enough to be made a ground for exposing to *extraordinary* risk the lives of brave and valuable men. The magnetic pole, though not attained, will yet be pointed to by distinct and unequivocal indications; viz. by the approximation of the dip to 90°; and by the convergence of the magnetic meridians on all sides towards it. If such convergence be observed over any considerable region, the place of the pole may thence be deduced, though its locality may be inaccessible.

M. Gauss, from theoretical considerations, has recently assigned a probable position in lon. 146° E., lat. 66° S., to the southern magnetic pole, denying the existence of two poles of the same name, in either hemisphere, which, as he justly remarks, would entail the necessity of admitting also a third point, having some of the chief characters of such a pole intermediate between them. That this is so, may be made obvious without following out his somewhat intricate demonstration, by simply considering, that if a needle be transported from one such pole to another of the same name, it will *begin* to deviate from perpendicularity *towards* the pole it has quitted, and will end in attaining perpendicularity again, after pointing in the latter part of its progress obliquely *towards the pole to which it is moving,* a sequence of things impossible without an intermediate passage through the perpendicular direction.

It is not improbable that the point indicated by M. Gauss will prove accessible; at all events it cannot but be approachable sufficiently near to test by the convergence of meridians the truth of the indication; and as his theory gives within very moderate limits of error the true place of the northern pole, and otherwise represents the magnetic elements in every explored region with considerable approximation, it is but reasonable to recommend this as a distinct point to be decided in Captain Ross's voyages. Should the decision be in the negative, i. e. should none of the indications characterizing the near vicinity of the magnetic pole occur in that region, it will be to be sought; and a knowledge of its real locality will be one of the distinct scientific results which may be confidently hoped from this Expedition, and which can only be attained by circumnavigating the antarctic pole compass in hand.

The actual attainment of a *focus* of maximum intensity is rendered difficult by the want of some distinct character by which it can be known, previous to trial, in which direction to proceed, when after increasing to a certain point the intensity begins again to diminish. The best rule to be given, would be (supposing circumstances would permit it) on perceiving the intensity to have become nearly stationary in its amount, to turn short and pursue a course at right angles to that just before followed, when a change could not fail to occur, and indicate by its direction towards which side the focus in question were situated.

Another, and as it would appear, a better mode of conducting such a research, would be, when in the presumed neighbourhood of a focus of maximum intensity, to run down two parallels of latitude or two arcs of meridians separated by an interval of moderate extent, observing all the way in each, by which observations, when compared, the concavities of the isodynamic lines would become apparent, and perpendiculars to the chords, intersecting in or near the foci, might be drawn.

Two foci or points of maximum *total* intensity are indicated by the general course of the lines in Major Sabine's chart in the Southern Hemisphere, one about long. 140° E., lat. 47° S., the other more obscurely in long. 235° E., lat. 60° S., or thereabouts. Both these points are certainly accessible; and as the course of the Expedition will lead not far from each of them, they might be visited with advantage by a course calculated to lead directly across the isodynamic ovals surrounding them.

Pursuing the course of the isodynamic lines in the chart above mentioned, it appears that one of the two points of *minimum* total intensity, which must exist, if that chart be correct, may be looked for nearly about lat. 25° S., long. 12° W., and that the intensity at that point is probably the least which occurs over the whole globe. Now this point does not lie much out of the direct course usually pursued by vessels going to the Cape. It would therefore appear desirable to pass directly over it, were it only for the sake of determining by direct measure the least magnetic intensity at present existing on the earth, an element not unlikely to prove of importance in the further progress of theoretical investigation. Excellent opportunities will be afforded for the investigation of all these points, and for making out the true form of the isodynamic ovals of the South Atlantic, both in beating up for St. Helena, and in the passage from thence to the Cape; in the course of which, the point of least intensity will, almost of necessity, have to be crossed, or at least approached very near.

Nor is the theoretical line indicated by Gauss as dividing the northern and southern regions, in which free magnetism may be regarded as superficially distributed, undeserving of attention. That line cuts the equator in 6° east longitude, being inclined thereto (supposing it a great circle) 15°, by which quantity it recedes from the equator northward in going towards the west of the point of intersection. Observations made at points lying in the course of this line may hereafter prove to possess a value not at present contemplated.

As a theoretical datum, the horizontal intensity has been recommended by Gauss, in preference to the total, not only as being concluded from observations susceptible of great precision, but as affording immediate facilities for calculation. As it cannot now be long before the desideratum of a chart of the horizontal intensity is supplied, the maxima and minima of this element may also deserve especial inquiry, and may be ascertained in the manner above pointed out.

The maxima of horizontal intensity are at present undetermined by any direct observation. They must of necessity, however, lie in lower magnetic latitudes than those of the total intensity, as its minima must in higher; and from such imperfect means as we have of judging, the conjectural situations of the maxima may be stated as occurring in

20° N.	80° E.	I.
7 N.	260 E.	II.
3 S.	130 E.	III.
10 S.	180 E.	IV.

Observations have been made of the horizontal intensity in the vicinities of II. and III., and are decidedly the highest which have been observed anywhere.

In general, in the choice of stations for determining the values of the three magnetic elements, it should be borne in mind, that the value of each new station is directly proportional to its remoteness from those already known. Should any doubt arise, therefore, as to the greater or less eligibility of particular points, a reference to the existing magnetic maps and charts, by showing where the known points of observation are most sparingly distributed, will decide it.

For such magnetic determinations as those above contemplated, the instruments hitherto in ordinary use, with the addition of Mr. Fox's apparatus for the statical determination of the intensity, will suffice; the number of the sea observations compensating for their possible want of exactness. The determinations which belong to the second branch of our subject,—viz. those of the secular changes, of the diurnal and other periodical variations, and of the momentary fluctuations of the magnetic forces,—require, in the present state of our knowledge, the use of those more refined instruments recently introduced, and to be presently described.

The variations to which the earth's magnetic force is subject, at a given place, may be classed under three heads, namely, 1. the *irregular* variations, or those which *apparently* observe no law ; 2. the *periodical* variations, whose amount is a function of the *hour angle* of the sun, or of its *longitude* ; and 3. the *secular* variations, which are either slowly progressive, or else return to their former values in periods of very great and unknown magnitude.

The recent discoveries connected with the *irregular* variations of the magnetic declination, have given to this class of changes a prominent interest. In the year 1818 M. Arago made, at the Observatory of Paris, a valuable and extensive series of observations on the declination changes ; and M. Kupffer having about the same time undertaken a similar research at Cazan, a comparison of the results led to the discovery that the perturbations of the needle were *synchronous* at the two places, although these places differed from one another by more than forty-seven degrees of longitude. This seems to have been the first recognition of a phenomenon, which now, in the hands of Gauss and those who are labouring with him, appears likely to receive a full elucidation.

To pursue this phenomenon successfully, and to promote in other directions the theory of terrestrial magnetism, it was necessary to extend and vary the stations of observation, and to adopt at all a common plan. Such a system of simultaneous observations was organized by Von Humboldt in the year 1827. Magnetic stations were established at Berlin and Freyberg : and the Imperial Academy of Russia entering with zeal into the project, the chain of stations was carried over the whole of that colossal empire. Magnetic *houses* were erected at Petersburg and at Cazan ; and magnetic instruments were placed, and regular observations commenced, at Moscow, at Sitka, at Nicolajeff in the Crimea, at Barnaoul and Nertschinsk in Siberia, and even at Pekin. The plan of observation was definitely organized in 1830 ; and simultaneous observations were made seven times in the year, at intervals of an hour for the space of forty-four hours.

In 1834 the illustrious Gauss turned his attention to the subject of terrestrial magnetism ; and having contrived instruments which were capable of yielding results of an accuracy before unthought of in magnetic researches, he proceeded to inquire into the simultaneous movements of the horizontal needle at distant places. At the very outset of his inquiry he discovered the fact, that the synchronism of the perturbations was not confined (as had been hitherto imagined) to the larger and extraordinary changes ; but that even the minutest deviation at one place of observation had its counterpart at the other. Gauss was thus led to organize a plan of simultaneous observations, not at intervals of an hour, but at the short intervals of five minutes. These were carried on through twenty-four hours six* times

* Recently reduced to *four*.

in the year; and magnetic stations taking part in the system were established at Altona, Augsburg, Berlin, Bonn, Brunswick, Breda, Breslau, Cassel, Copenhagen, Dublin, Freyberg, Göttingen, Greenwich, Halle, Kazan, Cracow, Leipsic, Milan, Marburg, Munich, Naples, St. Petersburg, and Upsala.

Extensive as this plan appears, there is much yet remaining to be accomplished. The stations, numerous as they are, embrace but a small portion of the earth's surface; and what is of yet more importance, none of them are situated in the neighbourhood of those *singular points* or curves on the earth's surface, where the *magnitude* of the changes may be expected to be excessive, and perhaps even their *direction* inverted. In short, a wider system of observation is required to determine whether the amount of the changes (which is found to be very different in different places) is dependent simply on the *geographical* or on the *magnetic* co-ordinates of the place; whether, in fact, the variation in that amount be due to the greater or less distance of a disturbing centre, or to the modifying effect of the mean magnetic force of the place, or to both causes acting conjointly. In another respect also, the plan of the simultaneous observations admits of a greater extension. Until lately the movements observed have been only those of the magnetic *declination*, although there can be no doubt that the *inclination* and the *intensity* are subject to similar perturbations. Recently, at many of the German stations, the *horizontal component* of the intensity has been observed, as well as the declination; but the determination of another element is yet required, before we are possessed of all the data necessary in this most interesting research.

The magnetic observatories about to be established in the British Colonies, by the liberality of the Government, and of the East India Company, will (it is hoped) supply in a great measure these desiderata. The stations are widely scattered over the earth's surface, and are situated at points of prominent interest with regard to the Isodynamic and Isoclinal lines. The point of maximum intensity in the northern hemisphere is *in* Canada; the corresponding maximum in the southern hemisphere is *near* Van Diemen's Land; St. Helena is close to the line of *minimum intensity*; and the Cape of Good Hope is of importance on account of its southern latitude. Again, in India, Madras and Sincapore are in the neighbourhood of the lines both of *minimum intensity* and of *no dip*, which in this region of the globe approach one another; and Semla, in the Himalaya mountains, is a station of interest and importance on account of its great elevation. At each observatory the changes of the *vertical component* of the magnetic force will be observed, as well as those of the *horizontal component* and *declination*; and the variations of the two components of the force being known, those of the *inclination* and of the *force* itself are readily deduced. The simultaneous observations of these three elements will be made at numerous and stated periods, and there is every reason to hope that the directors of many of the European observatories will take part in the combined system.

But interesting as these phenomena are, they form but a small part of the proper business of an observatory. The *regular* changes (both periodic and secular) are no less important than the irregular; and they are certainly those by which a patient inductive inquirer would seek to ascend to general laws. Even the empirical expression of the laws of these changes cannot fail to be of the utmost value, as furnishing a correction to the absolute values of the magnetic elements, and thereby reducing them to their mean amount.

The hourly changes of the *declination* have been frequently and attentively observed; but with respect to the periodical variations of the other two elements, our information is as yet very scanty. The determination of these variations will form an important part of the duty of the magnetic observatories; and from the accuracy of which the observations are susceptible, and the extent which it is proposed to give them, there can be no doubt that a very exact knowledge of the empirical laws will be the result.

With respect to the *secular* variations, it might perhaps be doubted whether the limited time during which the observatories will be in operation is adequate to their determination. But it should be kept in mind that the monthly mean corresponding to *each hour of observation* will furnish a separate result; and that the number and accuracy of the results thus obtained may be such, as fully to compensate for the shortness of the interval through which they are followed. A beautiful example of such a result, deduced from three years' observation of the declination, is to be found in the first volume of Gauss's magnetical work, of which a translation is published in the fifth number of Taylor's Scientific Memoirs.

Allusion has been made above to a different system of magnetic elements from that usually chosen. Before proceeding further, therefore, it is necessary to state more fully what those elements are which have been taken as the immediate objects of research; and to describe the instruments which have been adopted for the purpose.

The elements on which the determination of the earth's magnetic force is usually based are, the *declination*, the *inclination*, and the *intensity*. If a vertical plane be conceived to pass through the direction of the force, that direction will be determined when its inclination to the horizon is given, as well as the angle which the plane itself forms with the meridian; and if, in addition to these quantities, we likewise know the number which expresses the ratio of the intensity of the force to some established unit, it is manifest that the force is completely determined.

For many purposes, however, and especially in the delicate researches connected with the *variations* of the magnetic force, a different system of elements is preferable. The intensity being resolved into two portions in the plane of the magnetic meridian, one of them *horizontal* and the other *vertical*, it is manifest that these two components may be substituted for the total intensity and the inclination; while, at the same time, their changes may be determined with far greater precision. The former variables are connected with the latter by the relations

$$X = R \cos \theta, \qquad Y = R \sin \theta;$$

in which R denotes the intensity, X and Y its horizontal and vertical components, and θ the inclination; and the variations of θ and R are expressed in terms of the variations of X and Y by the formulæ:

$$\Delta \theta = \tfrac{1}{2} \sin 2\,\theta \left(\frac{\Delta Y}{Y} - \frac{\Delta X}{X} \right);$$

$$\frac{\Delta R}{R} = \cos^2 \theta \frac{\Delta X}{X} + \sin^2 \theta \frac{\Delta Y}{Y}.$$

As the instruments furnished to the fixed observatories, and to the Naval Expedition, for the observation of these elements are, for the most part, novel in form, it will be useful to give a somewhat detailed account of their construction and various adjustments, before entering on the plan of observation to be pursued.

DECLINATION MAGNETOMETER.

Construction.—The essential part of the declination magnetometer is a magnet bar, suspended by fibres of untwisted silk, and inclosed in a box, to protect it from the agitation of the air. The bar is a rectangular parallelopiped, 15 inches in length, $\frac{7}{8}$ths of an inch in breadth, and $\frac{1}{4}$th of an inch in thickness. In addition to the stirrup by which the bar is suspended, it is furnished with two sliding pieces, one near each end. One of these pieces contains an achromatic lens, and the other a finely divided scale of glass; the scale being adjusted to the focus of the lens, it is manifest that the apparatus forms a moving collimator, and that its absolute position at any instant, as well as its changes of position from one instant to another, may be read off by a telescope at a distance. The aperture of the lens of this collimator is $1\frac{1}{4}$ inch, and its focal length about 12 inches. Each division of the scale is $\frac{1}{383}$th part of an inch; and the corresponding angular quantity is about 43 seconds.

To the suspension thread is attached a small cylindrical bar, the ends of which are of smaller diameter, and support the stirrup which carries the magnet. The apertures in the stirrup, by which it hangs on the cylinder, are of the form of inverted Y s, so that the bearing points are invariable. A second pair of apertures at the other side of the magnet, serves for the purpose of *inversal*; and care has been taken to render the lines connecting the bearing points of each pair of Y s parallel, so that there may be no difference in the amount of torsion of the thread in the two positions of the stirrup. The two pairs of apertures are at different distances from the magnet, in order that the line of collimation may remain nearly at the same height on inversal, and thus it may not be necessary to alter the length of the suspension thread. The stirrup, and the other sliding pieces, are formed of gun metal.

For the purpose of taking out the torsion of the suspension thread, the apparatus is furnished with a *detorsion bar*, which (with its appendages) is of the same weight as the magnet. It is a rectangular bar of gun-metal, furnished with a stirrup and collimator similar to those of the magnet. A rectangular aperture in the middle receives a small magnet, the use of which is to impart a slight directive force to the suspended bar, and without which the final adjustment of detorsion would be tedious and difficult.

The frame-work of the instrument consists of two pillars of copper, 35 inches in height, firmly screwed to a massive marble base. These pillars are connected by two cross pieces of wood, one at the top, and the other 7 inches from the bottom. In the centre of the top piece is the suspension apparatus, and a divided circle used in determining the amount of torsion of the thread. A glass tube (between this and the middle of the lower cross piece) incloses the suspension thread; and a glass cap at top covers the suspension apparatus, and completes the inclosure of the instrument.

The box is cylindrical, its dimensions being 20 inches in diameter by 7 inches in depth. It rests upon the marble slab, and encompasses the pillars; and it is so contrived as to be raised, when necessary, for the purpose of manipulation. There are two apertures in the box, opposite to each other. The aperture in front, used for reading, is covered with a circular piece of parallel glass, attached to a rectangular frame of wood which moves in dovetails; the prismatic error of the glass (if any) is corrected by simply reversing the slider in the dovetails. The opposite aperture is for the illumination the scale.

In addition to the parts abovementioned, the instrument is provided with a second magnet, of the same dimensions as the first, to be used in measurements of absolute intensity; a thermometer, the bulb of which enters the box, in order to determine the interior temperature; and a copper ring, for the purpose of checking the vibrations*.

* The declination magnetometers provided for the Antarctic expedition differ from that above described in one or two particulars, which have been necessarily varied in order to enable the observer to read off *very great* deviations.

The magnet has a second stirrup, which is furnished with a mirror, for the purpose of reading the declination changes *by reflexion* after the method of Gauss. The mirror is attached to a cross, which is fixed to the stirrup; it is kept in its place by three small screws, the heads of which project and hold it; the plane of the mirror may be adjusted by the movement of these screws. The deviation of the line of collimator (which, in this case, is the normal to the surface of the mirror) from the magnetic axis of the bar, is ascertained by *inversal*, the stirrup being provided with a second pair of apertures, in the form of inverted Y's, for the purpose.

There are two graduated scales to be used with the mirror. The first of these is a *straight scale*, similar to that of Gauss, to be used for moderately large variations. This scale is 4 feet long, and the magnitude of each division is ·04082 of an inch. Every tenth division is numbered 1, 2, 3, &c. up to 100. The divisions are engraved and printed on paper which is parted on a slip of wood.

The second scale is graduated on a *complete circle*, 6 feet in diameter, and is to be used when the changes (regular or irregular) are excessive. The circle is of wood, and is in the shape of a flat ring, 9 inches in breadth, formed in segments

Adjustment.—The instrument having been placed on its support, the base is to be levelled, and the whole then fixed in its place. The levelling of the base may conveniently be performed by the aid of a plumb-line hanging in the place of the suspension thread; but no great precision is required in this operation, the chief object of which is that the suspension thread may occupy the middle of the tube, and that the magnet may be central with regard to its support. The suspension thread is then to be formed, and attached at one extremity to the roller of the suspension apparatus, and at the other to the small cylinder which is to bear the stirrup and magnet. Sixteen fibres* of untwisted-silk are sufficient to bear double the load without breaking, and will be found to form in other respects a convenient suspension.

These preparations being made, the adjustments are the following:

1. The sliders being placed on the magnet, the scale is to be adjusted to the focus of the lens, and in such a manner that the centre of gravity of the sliders may be near the middle of the bar. The adjustment to focus has been already made by the artist, and the corresponding distances of the sliders measured; they will be found in Table I.

2. The magnet is to be connected with the suspension thread by means of the stirrup, and to be moved in the stirrup until it assumes the horizontal position. This adjustment may be conveniently effected by means of the image of the magnet, reflected from the surface of water or mercury, the object and its reflected image being parallel when the former is horizontal. The stirrup is then fastened by its screws, and the magnet wound up to the desired height. As the thread stretches considerably at first, allowance should be made for this in the height.

3.+ The magnet is then removed, and the unmagnetic bar (having its collimator similarly adjusted) is to be attached, without its small magnet, and allowed to swing for several hours. The bar having come to rest, or nearly so, its deviation from the magnetic meridian is to be *estimated*, and the moveable arm of the torsion circle turned

---

so as to preserve its figure. At the exterior of the ring is a raised edge (also built in segments), on the interior face of which the scale is parted. The scale itself is the same as the former; the numbering of the divisions (every tenth) proceeding from 0 to 100, and then commencing anew. Paper being liable to stretch considerably when moistened, the whole circle has been divided into arcs of 20°, so as to determine with accuracy the angular value of each division. This value is

The aperture in the box is a rectangle, 6 inches long by $2\frac{1}{2}$ inches high, and is covered by a piece of wood sliding in dovetails, having a glass window of the usual size. The glass-cover will be used (with the collimator) when the variations are moderate; the uncovered aperture (with the mirror) when they are large, but not excessive; and, when the variations are very great, the box may be lifted altogether, so as to allow the entire range of azimuth.

* Not the individual fibre of the silk-worm, but the compound fibre in the state in which it is prepared for spinning.

† It is obvious that this step of the adjustment may precede the 1st and 2nd, where a saving of time is important.

through the same angle in an opposite direction. The plane of detorsion then coincides, approximately, with the magnetic meridian.

4. The magnet is then to be substituted for the unmagnetic bar, and the telescope being directed towards the collimator, the point of the scale coinciding with the vertical wire is to be noted when the magnet is in the *direct* and *inverted* positions. Half the sum of these readings is the point of the scale corresponding to the magnetic axis of the magnet bar; and half their difference (converted into angular measure) is the deviation of the line of collimation of the telescope from the magnetic meridian. The telescope should be moved through this angle in the opposite direction.

5. In order to take out the remaining torsion of the thread, the magnet is again to be removed, and the unmagnetic bar (with its small magnet attached) substituted. The deviation of this bar from the magnetic meridian should then be read off on its divided scale, and the moveable arm of the torsion circle turned through a given angle in the opposite direction. The deviation being again read, a simple proportion will give the remaining angle of torsion; and the moveable arm being turned through this angle in the opposite direction, another observation will serve to verify the adjustment. The plane of detorsion then coincides with the magnetic meridian; and the magnet being replaced, the instrument is ready for use.

Observations.—The observations to be made with this instrument are, 1. of the *absolute declination*; 2. of the *variations of the declination*; and 3. of the *absolute intensity*.

For measurements of the *absolute declination* each observatory is furnished with a small transit instrument having an azimuth circle. This instrument being placed in the magnetic meridian of the declination instrument, the point of the scale coinciding with the central wire of the transit telescope is to be observed; the interval between this point and the point corresponding to the magnetic axis of the bar, converted into angular measure, is the deviation, D, of the line of collimation of the transit telescope from the magnetic meridian. The verniers of the horizontal circle being then read, the telescope is turned, and its central wire made to bisect a distant mark, whose azimuth, Z, has been accurately determined. If A denote the angle read off on the horizontal circle, it is manifest that the angle between the magnetic and the astronomical meridians is

$$A + Z + D,$$

Z and D being affected with their proper signs. The angle Z is supposed to have been previously determined by the help of the transit instrument.

The division of the scale corresponding to the magnetic axis of the bar is to be considered as the *zero point*, and it must be determined with great exactness. It is obvious that this point will be given by the mean of two readings of the scale, with the magnet in the *erect* and *inverted* positions, provided that care has been taken to eliminate the declination changes which may occur in the interval of the two parts of the observation. The obvious method of effecting this elimination is to determine the amount of the declination change, by means of an auxiliary apparatus, and to apply it as a correction to the second result. The same thing may, however, be effected by taking a *series of readings* of the declination instrument alone, with the bar alternately erect and inverted ; the time chosen for observation being one in which the declination changes are small and regular, and the successive readings being made as rapidly as possible. By comparing each result with the *mean of the preceding and subsequent*, and then taking the mean of all these partial means, a very accurate determination may be made.

As a sample of such a determination, we may take the following observation, made at the Dublin Observatory, August 10, 1839. The first column of numbers contains the *actual* readings of the scale; the second the means of the preceding and subsequent readings ; and the third the means derived from the combination of these last with the intermediate reading.

I. Reversed	157·0		
II. Direct ..	193·2		
Observations interrupted.			
III. Reversed	169·6		
IV. Direct .	182·0	168·8	175·4
V. Reversed	168·0	182·3	175·2
VI. Direct ..	182·6	166·1	174·4
VII. Reversed	164·2		

Combining the three means in the last column with the number 175·1 deducted from I. and II., the final mean is 175·0.

The following observation, made at the Dublin Observatory, on the 10th of August, 1839, will illustrate the preceding method of determining the absolue declination.

In this Observatory the transit telescope and the theodolite are *distinct* instruments. The transit telescope is fixed. The centre of the theodolite is placed in the meridian line of the transit, and at the point where this line is cut by the magnetic meridian of the declination instrument, and the absolute declination is obtained by referring the telescope of the theodolite first to the line of collimation of the magnet, and then to that of the transit telescope.

It will be seen from the preceding table that the mean of the readings III. V. VII., in the inverted position of the bar, which in this instrument was the ordinary one, is 167·3 ; the mean time of observation being 1^h 40^m P. M., which corresponds nearly to the maximum declination of the day. But it has been already shown, that the *zero point* of the scale is 175·0, and the difference, 7·7, multiplied into 43″·22 (the angle corresponding to a *single* division) gives, for the deviation of the line of collimation of the telescope from the *magnetic meridian*,

$$D = - 5' 32''\cdot8.$$

The angle read off on the limb of the theodolite was 150° 30′.

The telescope of the theodolite was then directed to the object-glass of the transit instrument, and its line of collimation brought into the *astronomical* meridian by making the image of the vertical wire coincide with that of the middle wire of the transit. The reading of the limb was then found to be 358° 15′ 50″, and subtracting 180° (the magnet being to the north and the transit telescope to the south of the theodolite) the *true north* corresponds to the angle 178° 15′ 50″ on the limb. The difference between this and the angle 150° 30′, corresponding to the *magnetic north*, is

$$A = 27° 45' 50''.$$

Hence, as in this case $Z = 0$, the absolute declination is

$$A + D = 27° 40' 17''\cdot2.$$

If, instead of the *actual* declination at any moment we desired the *mean* declination of the day or of the month, we should employ (instead of the actual reading of the scale, 167·3) the corresponding mean result. We should thus obtain a new value of D, differing from the former by the amount of the declination change.

In the observations about to be established by Her Majesty's Government, the declination changes will be regularly observed with a *fixed telescope*, attached to a stone pillar, or to a firm pedestal of wood resting on solid masonry unconnected with the floor. Here then, instead of referring the transit telescope *directly* to the magnetic meridian by means of the moving collimator, the same result will be obtained, and probably in a better manner, by referring it to the line of collimation of the fixed telescope. For this purpose it is only necessary to employ this telescope as a collimator, the instrument being *reversed* in its Y supports, if necessary. A fixed collimator may also be conveniently substituted for the distant mark. This mode of observation has the advantage of connecting the absolute determination directly with the regular series of observations; and it is manifest that it is sufficient, without any other means, to determine whether any, and what changes may have occurred in the position of the fixed telescope.

In observing the *declination changes* the fixed telescope is alone employed. The observation consists simply in noting the point of the scale coinciding with the vertical wire, at three successive limits of the arc of vibration. The three readings being denoted by a, b, c, the mean point of the scale corresponding to the time of the middle observation is

$$\tfrac{1}{4}(a + 2b + c).$$

This mode of observation is sufficient where the observer is not limited to a *precise moment* of observation. Otherwise the more exact method pointed out by Gauss is to be preferred*.

The changes of position of the scale may be converted into angular measure, the angle corresponding to one division being known. In general, however, this reduction will only be required in the monthly mean results

Before the true changes of the declination can be deduced from the observed readings, it is necessary to apply a correction depending upon the force of torsion of the suspension thread. For supposing that the plane of detorsion has been brought (by the adjustments above described) to coincide with the magnetic meridian, it is manifest that on every deviation of the magnet from that of its mean position, the torsion force will be brought into play; and as this force tends to bring back the magnet to the mean position, the apparent deviations must be less than the true. The ratio of the torsion force to the magnetic directive force is experimentally determined by turning the moveable arm of the torsion circle through any given large angle (for example 90°), and observing the corresponding angle through which the magnet is deflected. Let u denote the latter angle, and w the former; then the ratio in question is

$$\frac{H}{F} = \frac{u}{w - v};$$

in which H is the coefficient of the torsion force, and F the moment arising from the action of the earth's magnetic force upon the free magnetism of the bar, the direction of the action being supposed to be perpendicular to its magnetic axis. The ratio of the two forces being thus found, the true declination changes are deduced from the apparent, by multiplying them by the coefficient

$$1 + \frac{H}{F}.$$

In order to obtain an exact result by the mode of experiment above described, it is necessary that the *actual* changes of the declination which may occur in the interval of the two readings, should be eliminated. The obvious method of accomplishing this, is to observe the declination changes *simultaneously* with a second apparatus. If such means, however, should not be at hand, the object may be attained by making a *series* of readings with the vernier of the torsion circle alternately in two fixed positions (for example + 90° and − 90°); the ·mean result will be independent of the declination changes, provided the progress of these changes has been gradual in the interval of the experiment.

The experiments necessary to determine the *absolute intensity* of terrestrial magnetism are of two kinds,—experiments of *deflection*

---

* See Taylor's Scientific Memoirs, vol. ii. part v. p. 44. *et seq.*

and experiments of *vibration*. The former of these gives the *ratio* of the horizontal component of the earth's magnetic force to the moment of free magnetism of the deflecting bar; the latter determines the *product* of the same quantities.

Deflection.—The deflecting bar is to be placed at right angles to the magnetic meridian, and in the line drawn perpendicularly through the centre of the declination bar. Its centre is to be placed, successively, at *two* different distances on this line; and in each position the observer is to note the angle of deflection produced by its action upon the suspended magnet of the declination instrument, the north end of the deflecting bar being placed, successively, towards the *east* and towards the *west*. Half the difference of the readings with the north end, east and west, converted into angular measure, is the deflection sought. The experiments are then to be repeated on the *other side* of the suspended magnet, and at the *same distances*, so that each angle of deflection is the mean of four observed results.

Let r and r' denote the two distances, u and u' the corresponding angles of deflection. Also let X denote, as before, the horizontal part of the earth's magnetic force, and m the moment of free magnetism of the deflecting bar. Then the ratio of these quantities is given by the following formula:

$$\frac{m}{X} = \frac{r'^5 \tan u' - r^5 \tan u}{2(r'^2 - r^2)}.$$

The quantity so obtained is to be corrected for the torsion force of the suspension thread of the declination magnetometer. This is done by multiplying it by the number $1 + \dfrac{H}{F}$.

In choosing the distances of the deflecting bar, we should take as the smaller that which produces a deflection nearly amounting to the entire limit of the scale, provided it be not less than four times the length of the bar. The other should be greater than this in the ratio of $\sqrt{3}$ to 1, nearly. The distances themselves should be measured with great accuracy, and expressed in feet and decimals of a foot. For the purpose of this measurement, each observatory is furnished with a standard yard and a beam compass.

Vibration.—The declination bar being now removed, the deflecting bar is to be placed in a temporary stirrup of silk or wire, and so attached to the cylinder of the suspension thread. Its time of vibration is now to be determined with accuracy, from at least 100 oscillations. This may be done by placing a fine mark (as a piece of fine silver wire) on the front end of the bar, and noting the time of passage across the fixed wire of the reading telescope. The telescope is for this purpose furnished with an additional object lens, which is to be placed over the other, so as to adapt the instrument to near distances.

The time being observed, and the *moment of inertia* of the bar calculated, the *product* of the force of the earth and the moment of free magnetism of the bar is given by the formula

$$X m = \frac{\pi^2 K}{T^2} ;$$

in which π denotes the ratio of the circumference of a circle to its diameter, K the moment of inertia, and T the time of vibration.

The moment of inertia, K, is given by the formula

$$K = \frac{a^2 + b^2}{12} M ;$$

a and b denoting the length and breadth of the bar, and M its *mass*.

In order to correct the torsion force of the suspension thread, the time of vibration deduced from experiment must be multiplied by

$$\sqrt{1 + \frac{H}{F}} ;$$ and therefore the square of the time by $1 + \frac{H}{F}$.

Again, inasmuch as these experiments necessarily occupy a considerable time, precision requires that we should apply a correction for the changes of the intensity which may occur in the course of the observation. In other words, we must reduce the observed value of $X m$ (at the time of the experiment of vibration) to that which it had at the time of the experiment of deflection. This may at once be done by the aid of the horizontal force magnometer, inasmuch as that instrument gives immediately the changes of X m. In this case, however,—that is, when there is a second magnet in the same room,—the deduced value of X will be (not the earth's magnetic form) but the resultant of that force and the force of the second magnet; and both experiment and calculation will be required to deduce the former. It is accordingly safer, perhaps, to remove the second magnet for the time to another apartment, and to determine the changes of the horizontal force by observing the time of vibration of this bar simultaneously with the two parts of the experiment above described. Thus, let t' be time of vibration during the experiment of deflection, t the time during the experiment of vibration, then the corrected time of the deflected bar is

$$T' = T \frac{t'}{t}.$$

The values of $\frac{m}{X}$ and of $m X$ being known, that of X is at once obtained by elimination. Let $\frac{m}{X} = A$, $m X = B$, then it is evident that

$$X + \sqrt{\frac{B}{A}}.$$

The number thus obtained for the force of the earth's magnetism expresses the ratio which that force bears to the *unit of force*,—the unit of force being that which, acting on the unit of *mass*, through the unit of *time*, generates in it the unit of velocity. These units are entirely arbitrary; but for the sake of convenience in comparison, it is desirable that they should be the same in all the observations which shall be made according to this system. For the unit of mass, then, we may take a *grain*; for the unit of time a *second*; and, if a *foot* be taken as the unit of space, the unit of velocity will be that of one foot per second.

As the magnetic force operates effectively only on the free or un-combined elements of the magnetic fluid, we are to understand, by the earth's magnetic force, its action on the elementary unit of free magnetism; and we must take for that unit the quantity of free magnetism, which acting on another equal quantity at the unit of distance, exerts an effect equal to the unit of force already defined.

The following example, taken from Gauss's memoir, '*Intensitas vis Terrestris ad mensuram absolutam revelata*,' will serve to illustrate the preceding rules.

The experiments were made in two apparatuses, denoted by the letters A and B, and with three bars, distinguished by the numbers 1, 2, 3.

In the first place, the oscillation of bar 1 in the apparatus A, and of bar 2 in the apparatus B, were simultaneously observed. The time of a single oscillation, reduced to infinitely small arcs, was found to be

$$\text{for bar 1} \quad \dots \quad 15^s\cdot22450,$$
$$\text{for bar 2} \quad \dots \quad 17^\cdot\ 29995;$$

the former being deducted from 305 oscillations, the latter from 264.

Bar 3 being then suspended in the apparatus A, bar 1 was placed in the right line perpendicular to the magnetic meridian, both on the east and west side of the suspended bar (and in both cases with the north end east and west successively), and the deflection of bar 3 was observed in each position of bar 1. These experiments were repeated for two different distances, R, and with the following values of deflection, u:

$$R = 1^m\cdot2, \quad u = 3^\circ\ 42'\ 19''\cdot4;$$
$$R' = 1\ \cdot6, \quad u' = 1\ \ 34\ \ 19\ \cdot3.$$

During these experiments the oscillations of bar 2 were observed in the apparatus B. The time of a single oscillation, deduced from 414 oscillations, and corresponding to the mean time of the experiments of deflection, was $17^s\cdot29484$. The times were observed with a chronometer, whose daily rate was $-14^s\cdot24$.

The values of $\dfrac{H}{F}$, for bars 1 and 3, were found to be $\dfrac{1}{597\cdot4}$ and $\dfrac{1}{721\cdot6}$ respectively.

The moment of inertia of bar 1 was

$$K = 4328732400,$$

taking a *millimetre* and a *milligramme* as the units of distance and mass.

Now, to calculate the results of these experiments:—the inequality of the times of oscillation of bar 2 proves that a slight variation of the terrestrial magnetic intensity had taken place in the interval of the two parts of the observation. Accordingly, we have to reduce the observed time of oscillation of bar 1, to that corresponding to the mean state of terrestrial magnetism during the second part of the observation. This time requires also a second reduction for the chronometer's rate, and a third for the torsion of the thread. The reduced time thus comes out

$$T = 15 \cdot 22450 \times \frac{17 \cdot 29484}{17 \cdot 29995} \times \frac{86400}{86385 \cdot 76} \times \sqrt{\frac{598 \cdot 4}{597 \cdot 4}}$$

$$= 15 \cdot 23580.$$

$$\therefore m \, X = \frac{\pi^2 \, K}{T^2} = 179770600.$$

From the observed deflections we obtain

$$\frac{m}{X} = \frac{R'^5 \tan u' - R^5 \tan u}{2 \, (R'^2 - R^2)} = 56528100 \, ;$$

the millimetre being taken as the unit of distance; and correcting this quantity for the torsion of the three, by multiplying it by the coefficient $1 + \dfrac{H}{F} = \dfrac{722 \cdot 6}{721 \cdot 6}$,

$$\frac{m}{X} = 56606437.$$

From this, and the value of $m \, X$, we conclude

$$X = \sqrt{\frac{179770600}{56606437}} = 1 \cdot 782088.$$

The following table contains the interval of the sliders of the collimators, corresponding to focal adjustment; and also the arc values of one division of the scale in each instrument, expressed in decimals of a minute.

TABLE I.

No. of Instrument.	Observatory.	Interval of Sliders.	Arc value of one division.
		inches.	′
I.	H.M.S. Erebus	11·70	0·7267
II.	Van Diemen's Land	12·01	0·7085
III.	Montreal.	11·72	0·7208
IV.	Cape of Good Hope	11·18	0·7525
V.	St. Helena......	11·96	0·7108

Horizontal Force Magnetometer.

The instrument employed in determining the horizontal component of the earth's magnetic force is similar, in principle, to the
"*bifilar magnetometer*" of Gauss. It is a magnet bar, suspended by
two equidistant wires, or (more accurately) by two portions of the
same wire, the distance of whose bearing points is the same above
and below; by the rotation of the upper extremities of the wire
round their middle point, the magnet is maintained in a position at
right angles to the magnetic meridian.

It is manifest from the nature of this suspension, that the *weight*
of the suspended body will tend to bring it into the position in which
the two portions of the wire are in the *same plane* throughout. The
moment of the directive force is G sin v;—v denoting the angle
formed by the lines joining the bearing points above and below, or
the deviation from the plane of detorsion; and G being expressed by
the formula

$$G = W \frac{a^2}{l};$$

in which W denotes the weight of the suspended body, a half the interval of the wires, and l their length. The earth's *magnetic force*, on
the other hand, tends to bring the magnetic axis of the bar into the
magnetic meridian, with the force F sin u; in which u is the deviation
of the magnetic axis from the meridian, and F is the product of the
horizontal part of the earth's magnetic force into the moment of free
magnetism of the bar. The magnet being thus acted on by two
forces, will rest in the position in which their moments are equal.
When the instrument is so adjusted that $u = 90°$, or the magnet at
right angles to the magnetic meridian,

$$F = G \sin v;$$

and the ratio of the forces is known, when we know the angle v.
But as one of these forces is constant, and the other variable, it is
evident that the place of the magnet will vary around its mean position, and that the variations of angle are connected with the variations of the force. This connexion is expressed by the formula

$$\frac{\Delta F}{F} = - \cotan v \, \Delta u;$$

the angle Δu being expressed in parts of radius.

Construction.—The magnet bar is of the same dimensions as that of
the declination instrument. The collimator, by which its changes
of position are observed, is attached to the stirrup, and has a motion
in azimuth*. The suspending wire passes round a small grooved

---

* The horizontal force magnetometer belonging to H. M. S. Erebus is provided
with a *mirror* attached to the stirrup of the magnet, and *two scales*, similar to
those of the declination magnetometer. The mirror, however, has a movement
in azimuth, in the same manner as the collimator which it replaces.

wheel, on the axis of which the stirrup rests by inverted Y s; and the instrument is furnished with a series of such wheels, whose diameters increase in arithmetical progression, (the common difference being about $\frac{1}{20}$th of an inch,) for the purpose of varying the interval of the wires. The exact intervals, corresponding to each separate wheel, have been determined by the artist by accurate micrometrical measurements; they are given in Table III. The same interval is altered, at the upper extremity, by means of two screws (one right-handed and the other left-handed) cut in the same cylinder; the wires being lodged in the intervals of the threads, and their distance regulated by a micrometer head. The interval of the threads of this screw (which is precisely the same for all the instruments) is $\frac{2}{77}$ths, or ·02597 of an inch. The micrometer head is divided into 100 parts; and, as one revolution of the head corresponds to *two* threads of the screw, a single division is equivalent to ·0005194, or the $\frac{1}{2000}$th of an inch nearly. The micrometer head has been carefully adjusted by the artist, so that the index is at zero, when the interval of the wires is exactly half an inch.

The collimator, in this instrument, is inclosed in a light tube attached to the stirrup. The aperture of the lens is about $\frac{8}{10}$ths of an inch, and its focal length about 8 inches. The divisions of the scale are the same as in the collimator of the declination magnetometer; the corresponding arc values have been ascertained for each instrument by accurate experiment, and are given in Table II.

The larger parts of this apparatus,—the box, the framework, and the support,—are precisely similar to those of the declination magnetometer. In addition to the parts already described, the instrument is furnished with a spare magnet; a brass weight, required in determining the plane of detorsion of the wires relatively to the magnetic meridian; a thermometer, the bulb of which is within the box, for the purpose of ascertaining the interior temperature; and a copper ring used in checking the vibrations.

Adjustments.—The instrument being placed on its support, the base is to be levelled, and the whole apparatus fixed. Having then selected one of the small grooved wheels, and fixed it, temporarily, with its axis horizontal, the wire is to be passed round it; and the free extremities of the wire being passed through the corresponding holes in the suspension roller, placed beneath, weights are to be attached, and the two portions of the wire allowed to assume their natural position; the extremities may then be *fastened* to the roller, by introducing small wooden plugs in the holes. The parts are then to be inverted, and put in their proper places; the suspension apparatus resting on the divided circle, and the wire hanging down the tube.

The collimator (its scale having been previously adjusted to focus*) is to be screwed on to the stirrup, and the latter attached to the axis of the grooved wheel by means of its Y s. The magnet is then in-

---

* This adjustment has been already made by the artist.

troduced into the stirrup, and levelled; and the wires wound upon the roller, until the collimator is at the desired height.

These preparations being made, the adjustments are the following:

1. Determine experimentally the angle through which it is necessary to turn the moveable arm of the torsion circle, in order to deflect the magnet from the magnetic meridian to a position at right angles to it, the two positions being merely *estimated*. The cosine of this angle is, approximately, the ratio of the magnetic force to the torsion force, or the value of the fraction $\frac{F}{G}$. The nearer this ratio is to unity, the more delicate will be the instrument; practically, $\frac{9}{10}$ will be found a convenient value. If, on making the foregoing experiment, the ratio should be found to fall below, or to exceed the proper limits, the torsion force must be altered by introducing a different wheel, and making the corresponding alteration in the interval of the upper extremities of the wires.

2. The magnetic axis being brought, approximately, into the magnetic meridian, by turning the moveable arm of the torsion circle, the collimator is to be turned, by its independent motion, until some point about the middle of the scale coincides with the vertical wire of the fixed telescope. This point of the scale is to be noted in the usual manner.

3. The magnet is then to be removed, and the brass weight attached. Note the new point of the scale which coincides with the wire of the telescope. Then, if the magnet had been placed (in the previous experiment) in its *direct* position (i. e. north to north) the error of the plane of detorsion is

$$\left(\frac{G}{F}+1\right)v',$$

v' being the difference of the two readings, converted into angular measure. If, on the other hand, the magnet had been *reversed* (i. e. north end to south) the error is

$$\left(\frac{G}{F}-1\right)v''$$

The moveable arm of the torsion circle is then to be turned through this angle, in the opposite direction; and the magnetic axis will be in the magnetic meridian.

The difference of the two readings, corresponding to a given error, being much greater in the reversed than in the direct position of the magnet, it follows that the former affords a much more delicate method of making the desired adjustment.

4. The brass weight remaining attached, turn the moveable arm of the torsion circle through 90°. Then turn back the collimator, until some point about the middle of the scale coincides with the vertical wire of the fixed telescope; and note the reading.

5. Now remove the brass weight, and replace the magnet. The magnetic force of the earth will bring it back towards the magnetic

meridian, and the scale will be thrown out of the field of the telescope. Then turn the moveable arm of the torsion circle, until the point of the scale last noted is brought to coincide again with the wire of the telescope; the magnetic axis is then in the plane perpendicular to the magnetic meridian, and the adjustment is complete.

The following adjustment, made at the Dublin Magnetical Observatory, will serve to exemplify the foregoing description.

August 14.—Having attached the wire in the manner described, the wheel No. 5, whose diameter $= 0\cdot4607$ of an inch, was introduced, and the stirrup and weight appended. The upper extremities of the wire having been adjusted to the interval of *half an inch* (the zero point) by means of the micrometer, the correction to be made in the upper interval was, in parts of an inch,

$$0\cdot4607 - 0\cdot5000 = - 0\cdot0393;$$

and dividing this number by $\cdot0005194$, the fraction of an inch corresponding to a *single division* of the micrometer head, the resulting number, 76, expresses the *number of divisions* through which the micrometer head was to turned *backward*, so as to equalize the interval of the wires at top and bottom. The microscope was accordingly turned back from 100 or zero to the division numbered 24.

1. The magnet being now introduced into the stirrup, and th weight removed, it was found necessary to turn the moveable arm of the torsion circle through 151° 30′, in order to deflect the magnet from the magnetic meridian to a position at right angles to it, the two positions being known only approximately. Hence the approximate value of the fraction

$$\frac{F}{G} = \cos(151° 30′) = \cdot88.$$

2. The moveable arm of the torsion circle was then turned, until the magnetic axis was, approximately, in the magnetic meridian: and the reading of the torsion circle was found to be 260° 10′. The collimator was then turned, by its independent motion, until the division coinciding with the vertical wire of the fixed telescope was about the middle of the scale. The coinciding division was 140.

3. The magnet was now removed, and the brass weight attached; and the new coinciding division was observed to be 118. The difference of the two readings is 22, and multiplying 1′·0776 (the arc value of a single division) by this difference, the angle $v = 24′$. Consequently (the magnet having been placed in the *direct* position) the error of the plane of detorsion is

$$v\left(\frac{G}{F} + 1\right) = 24′ \times \frac{1\cdot88}{0\cdot88} = 51′.$$

Subsequent trials, however, showed that the error here deduced was greater than the truth; and that the two readings of the scale agreed, when the reading of the torsion circle was 260° 32′.

4. The brass weight being attached, the moveable arm of the torsion circle was turned through 90 degrees, so that its reading was

350° 32'. The collimator was then turned back, by its independent motion, until the coinciding division was about the middle of the circle. The reading of the circle was 134.

5. The brass weight was then removed, and the magnet replaced; the scale was consequently thrown out of the field of the telescope. The moveable arm of the torsion circle was turned further, in the same direction as before, until the division of the scale last noted, 134, again coincided with the wire of the telescope. The magnetic axis was then perpendicular to the magnetic meridian, and the adjustment was complete.

The reading of the torsion circle, after this step of the adjustment, was found to be 51° 2'; and consequently

$$v = 60° 30' \text{ and } \frac{F}{G} \sin v = \cdot8704.$$

Observations.—The observations to be made with this instrument are those of the *absolute* value of the *horizontal intensity*, and its *changes.*

From the explanation of the principle of the instrument, given above, it is manifest that it will serve to determine the moment of the force exerted by the earth upon the free magnetism of the suspended bar. Let X denote (as before) the horizontal part of the earth's magnetic force; m the moment of free magnetism of the bar; then

$$m\,X = F,$$

F having the same meaning as before (page 9). Hence, substituting the values of F and G, we have

$$m\,X = W\,\frac{a^2}{l}\sin v\,;$$

in which equation all the quantities of the second member may be obtained by direct measurement. The chief difficulty in this method consists in the determination of the quantity a, which should be known to a very small fractional part of its actual value. This difficulty has been overcome by the measuring apparatus connected with the suspension, which (as has been already stated) serves to determine the interval of the wires, at their upper extremity, to the $\frac{1}{2000}$th of an inch. The numbers given in Table III. for the lower interval, may be relied on to the same degree of accuracy. It is scarcely necessary to mention that the length of the wires, l, is to be measured between the points of contact above and below.

The *product* of the earth's magnetic force into the magnetic moment of the bar being thus known, the *ratio* of the same quantities is to be determined by removing the bar from its stirrup, and using it to *deflect* the suspended bar of the declination instrument, according to the known method devised by Gauss. The experiments of deflection may, however, be performed without the aid of the second magnetometer, by operating upon another bar placed in the *reverse* position. This method has even the advantage in point of delicacy;

but it labours under the disadvantage of requiring that the value of $\frac{F}{G}$ should be determined for the second bar.

The chief use of this apparatus is in observing the *variations* of the intensity. In these observations it is only necessary to note, at any moment, the point of the scale coinciding with the vertical wire of the fixed telescope, the mode of observing being precisely the same as in the other instrument. Let n be the number of divisions, and parts of a division, by which the reading at any moment differs from its mean value; then the corresponding variation of the angle (in parts of radius) is

$$\Delta u = n\,a;$$

a denoting the arc value (in parts of radius) corresponding to a single division. Substituting this in the formula of page 10, and making

$$k = a\,\mathrm{cotan}\,v,$$

we have

$$\frac{\Delta F}{F} = -k\,n;$$

The values of a have been determined for each of the instruments, and are given in Table II.

Thus, in the instrument in use in the Dublin Observatory, the angle corresponding to a single division of the scale is $= 1'\!\cdot\!0776$, so that $a = \cdot0003135$. And since, in the adjustment of this instrument it was found that $v = 60^\circ\ 30'$, we have

$$k = \cdot0003135 \times \mathrm{cotan}\ (60^\circ\ 30') = \cdot0001774.$$

The quantity F, in the preceding formula, is the product of the earth's magnetic force into the moment of free magnetism of the bar; and, as the latter quantity varies with the temperature, it is necessary to apply a correction, before we can infer the true changes of the earth's force. This correction is easily deduced. Since $F = X\,m$, there is

$$\frac{\Delta F}{F} = \frac{\Delta X}{X} + \frac{\Delta m}{m};$$

so that the correction to be applied, in order to deduce the value of $\frac{\Delta X}{X}$, is $-\frac{\Delta m}{m}$. Let t denote the temperature, in degrees of Fahrenheit; q the relative change of the magnetic moment corresponding to one degree; then

$$-\frac{\Delta m}{m} = q\,(t - 32).$$

Accordingly, the changes of the earth's force will be expressed by the formula

$$\frac{\Delta X}{X} = -k\,n + q\,(t - 32).$$

It is not necessary that these reductions should be applied to the individual results, except in cases of marked change, where it is desired to trace the progress of the actual phenomena. The results should be recorded as they are observed, in parts of the scale; and the reductions made in the monthly, or other mean values.

Table II. contains the arc values of one division of the scale, in each instrument, expressed in *decimals of a minute*; as also the same quantities reduced to *radius*, as the unit, by multiplying by the number 0002909.

TABLE II.

No. of Instrument.	Observatory.	Arc values of one division.	
		In Minutes.	In parts of Radius.
I.	H.M.S. Erebus	1·075	·0003127
II.	Van Diemen's Land	1·080	·0003142
III.	Montreal.... ...	1·074	·0003124
IV.	Cape of Good Hope	1·084	·0003153
V.	St. Helena ..	1·080	·0003142

Table III. contains the intervals of the axes of the wires corresponding to each wheel, in decimals of an inch; the wire used being that designated in commerce as "silver, fine 6."

TABLE III.

No. of Wheel.	I. H.M.S. Erebus.	II. Van Diemen's Land.	III. Montreal.	IV. Cape of Good Hope.	V. St. Helena.
1	·2536	·2549	·2529	·2542	·2536
2	·3032	·3058	·3055	·3055	·3065
3	·3529	·3516	·3529	·3497	·3513
4	·4058	·4088	·4078	·4052	·4071
5	·4562	·4555	·4581	·4555	·4545
6	·5055	·5071	·5042	·5055	·5058
7	·5555	·5604	·5588	·5565	·5591
8	·6071	·6071	·6071	·6097	·6081

VERTICAL FORCE MAGNETOMETER.

The instrument used in determining the changes of the *vertical component* of the magnetic force is a magnetic needle resting on agate planes, by knife-edges, and brought to the horizontal position by weights. From the changes of position of such a needle, the changes of the vertical force may be inferred, when we know the mean inclination at the place of observation, and the times of vibration of the needle in the vertical and in the horizontal planes. For it may be shown that

$$\frac{\Delta F}{F} = \frac{T'^2}{T^2} \cotan \theta \, \Delta \eta \,;$$

where $\Delta \eta$ denotes the change of the angle in parts of radius, θ the *inclination*, and T and T' the times of vibration of the needle in the *vertical* and *horizontal* planes respectively.

Construction.—The magnetic needle is 12 inches in length. It has a cross of wires at each extremity, attached by means of a small ring of copper; the interval of the crosses being 13 inches. The axis of the needle is formed into a *knife edge*, the edge being adjusted to pass as nearly as possible through the centre of gravity of the unloaded instrument. The weights by which the other adjustments are effected are small brass screws moving in fixed nuts, one on each arm; the axis of one of the screws being *parallel* to the magnetic axis of the needle, and that of the other *perpendicular* to it.

The agate planes upon which the needle rests are attached to a solid support of copper, which is firmly fixed to a massive marble base. In this support there is a provision for raising the needle off the planes, the contrivance for effecting this object being similar to that employed in the inclination instrument. The whole is covered with an oblong box of mahogany, in one side of which are two small glazed apertures, for the purpose of reading; the opposite side of the box is covered with plate glass. A thermometer, within the box, shows the temperature of the interior air; and a spirit level, attached to the marble base, serves to indicate any change of level which may occur in the instrument.

The position of the needle at any instant is observed by means of two micrometer microscopes, one opposite each end. These microscopes are supported on short pillars of copper, attached to the base of the instrument. They are so adjusted that one complete revolution of the micrometer screw corresponds to about 5 minutes of arc. The micrometer head is divided into 50 parts; and, consequently, the arc corresponding to a single division is about $0'\cdot1$.

In addition to these parts, the apparatus is provided with a brass bar of the same length as the magnet, (furnished, like it, with cross wires at the extremities, and knife-edge bearings,) for the purpose of determining the zero points of the micrometers; a brass scale, divided to $10'$, used in adjusting the value of their divisions; and a horizontal needle, to be employed in determining the azimuth of the vertical plane in which the needle moves.

Adjustments.—The following are the adjustments required in this instrument:

1. The instrument being placed on its support, in a suitable position with respect to the other two instruments, the azimuth of the plane in which the needle is to move may be adjusted in the following manner. The plane is made to coincide, in the first instance,

with the magnetic meridian, by means of the horizontal needle which moves upon a pivot fixed to the top of the scale. A small theodolite (or other instrument for measuring horizontal angles) is then placed on the base; and its telescope brought to bear on a distant mark. The telescope should then be moved through a horizontal angle equal to the intended azimuth of the instrument, but in an opposite direction. The base of the instrument is next to be turned, without disturbing the theodolite, until the mark is again bisected by the wires of the telescope: it is then in the required azimuth. The base should then be levelled, and permanently fixed.

2. The *fixed* wires of the microscopes are then to be adjusted to the same *horizontal* line. This is effected by means of the brass needle. This needle being placed upon the agate planes, by its knife-edges, and allowed to come to rest, it is manifest that the line joining the cross wires will be horizontal, provided it be perpendicular to the line joining the centre of gravity and the axis. To effect this latter adjustment, the needle (a great part of whose weight is disposed below the knife-edge) is furnished also with a small moveable weight. The test of the adjustment is similar to that of the corresponding adjustment of the ordinary balance. The moveable wire of one of the microscopes being brought to bisect the cross, if the adjustment is complete, it will bisect the cross at the other extremity upon reversal; if not, the position of the needle will indicate in what manner the weight is to be moved.

A horizontal line being thus obtained, the fixed wires of the microscopes are to be adjusted to it, by moving the capstan-headed screws with which they are connected.

3. The last adjustment is that of the magnetic needle to the horizontal position. To effect this adjustment the needle is furnished with two moving weights, one on each arm. These weights (it has been already stated) are screws moving in fixed nuts, one in a direction parallel to the magnetic axis of the needle, and the other in a direction at right angles to it. By the movement of the former the needle is brought to the horizontal position; and by that of the latter, the centre of gravity is made to approach the centre of motion, and the sensibility of the instrument thereby augmented.

Observations.—In observing the variations of the vertical force with this instrument, it is only necessary to bring the moveable wire of each micrometer to bisect the opposite cross of the needle; unless in seasons of disturbance, the needle will be found at each instant to have assumed its position of equilibrium. The interval between the fixed and moveable wires, expressed in angular measure, is the deviation of the needle from the horizontal position; and the changes of the vertical force are thence obtained by multiplying by a constant coefficient.

If n denote the number of divisions, and parts of a division, corresponding to the interval of the micrometer wires,

$$\Delta \eta = h\, a,$$

a denoting the angle (in parts of the radius) corresponding to a single division. Consequently, the changes of the force are expressed (as in the case of the other component) by the formula

$$\frac{\Delta F}{F} = k\,n\,;$$

in which the constant coefficient is

$$k = a \cot \theta \cdot \frac{T'^2}{T^2}$$

The quantity F in the preceding formula is the product of the vertical component of the earth's magnetic force multiplied by the moment of free magnetism of the needle, or

$$F = m\,Y\,;$$

accordingly the results thus deduced require a correction for the effects of temperature upon the quantity m. This correction is similar to that applied to the horizontal intensity, and the corrected expression of the changes of the vertical component is consequently

$$\frac{\Delta Y}{Y} = k\,n + q\,(t - 32)\,;$$

where t denotes the actual temperature (in degrees of Fahrenheit) at the time of observation, and q the relative change of the magnetic moment of the needle corresponding to one degree. As in the case of the other instruments, however, it is not in general necessary to apply these reductions to the individual results.

TIMES OF OBSERVATION.

The objects of inquiry in terrestrial magnetism may be naturally classed under two heads, according as they relate, 1. to the *absolute* values of the magnetic elements at a given epoch, or their mean values for a given period; or 2. to the *variations* which these elements undergo from one epoch to another. It will be convenient to consider separately the observations relating to these two branches of the subject.

Absolute Determinations.

By the method of observation which has been suggested for the *absolute declination*, every determination of the position of the declination bar is rendered absolute. We have only to consider the varying angle between the magnetic axis of the bar and the line of collimation of the fixed telescope, as a correction to be applied to the constant angle (already determined) between the latter line and the meridian. It is manifest that if the *fixity* of the line of collimation of the telescope could be depended on, a single determination of the latter angle would be sufficient. But this is not to be trusted for any considerable period; and it will be therefore necessary, from time to time, to refer the line of collimation of the telescope to the meridian, by means of the transit instrument. This observation

D

may be repeated *once a month*, or more frequently if any change in the position of the telescope be suspected.

In the case of the *intensity*, there is another source of error (besides that due to a change in the position of the instruments) which can only be guarded against by a repetition of *absolute* measurements. The magnetic moment of the magnet itself may alter; and the observations of intensity changes afford no means of separating this portion of the effect from that due to a change in the earth's magnetism. This separation can only be effected by means analogous to those employed in the determination of the absolute value of the horizontal intensity; and accordingly one or other (or both) of the methods proposed for this determination should be occasionally resorted to. It is desirable that this observation should be repeated *once in every month*; and more frequently, whenever the changes observed with the horizontal force magnetometer indicate, by their *progressive* character, a change in the magnetic moment of the suspended bar.

It would be easy, in theory, to devise a method by which the vertical force magnetometer might be made to serve in determining the absolute value of the vertical intensity. The means which at present offer themselves appear, however, to be surrounded with practical difficulties; and it seems safer to deduce this result *indirectly*. From the formulæ given in page 3, we have

$$Y = X \tan \theta;$$

so that if the inclination, θ, be known, and the horizontal intensity, X, determined in absolute measure, the vertical intensity, Y, is inferred.

For the purpose of observing the element θ, each observatory is furnished with an inclination instrument, the circle of which is $9\frac{1}{2}$ inches in diameter. The observation should be made in an open space, sufficiently remote from the magnets of the observatory, and from other disturbing influences; and a series of measures should be taken *simultaneously* with the two intensity magnetometers, for the purpose of eliminating the *changes of the inclination* which may occur in the course of the observation. As to the mode of observation, the best seems to be the usual one, the plane of the circle coinciding with the magnetic meridian; but for the purpose of testing the axles of the needles, and the divided limb of the instrument, it is desirable that some observations should be made in *various azimuths*, —for example, every 30° of the azimuth circle commencing with the magnetic meridian. The inclination is then inferred, from each pair of corresponding results, by the formula

$$\cotan^2 \theta = \cotan^2 \eta + \cotan^2 \eta';$$

η and η' being the observed angles of inclination in two planes at right angles to one another. Where the inclination is great (as in Canada), this method will serve to test only a limited portion of the circumference of the axle and limb. In this case the best course appears to be that pointed out by Major Sabine*, namely, to con-

---

* *Reports of the British Association*, vol. vii. p. 55.

vert one of the needles, temporarily, into a needle on Mayer's principle, by loading it with sealing-wax ; and to deduce the inclination, from the angles of position of the loaded needle, by the known formula of Mayer. The observations here suggested having been very carefully made, and the inclination changes eliminated in the manner above explained, the observed difference between the *mean* and the result obtained in the *magnetic meridian*, should be applied as a correction for the errors of axle and limb to all future observations made in the meridian.

These observations should be made at the same periods as those of the absolute horizontal intensity.

Variation of the Elements.

The *variations* of the magnetic elements are, 1. Those variations whose amount is a function of the *hour angle* of the sun, or of his *longitude*; and which return to their original values at the same hour in successive days, or the same season in successive years. These, from their analogy to the corresponding planetary inequalities, may be denominated *periodical.* 2. The variations, which are either continually *progressive,* or else return to their former values in long and unknown periods; these may in like manner be denominated *secular.* 3. The *irregular* variations, whose amount changes from one moment to another, and which observe (apparently) no law.

The *periodical* variations (with the exception of those of the *declination*) have hitherto been little studied; and, even in the case of the single element just mentioned, the results have scarcely gone beyond a general indication of the hours of maxima and minima, and of the changes of their amount with the season. The subject is nevertheless of the highest importance in a theoretical point of view. The phenomena depend, it is manifest, on the action of solar heat, operating probably through the medium of thermoelectric currents induced on the earth's surface. Beyond this rude guess, however, nothing is as yet known of the physical cause. It is even still a matter of speculation whether the solar influence be a *principal,* or only a *subordinate* cause, in the phenomena of terrestrial magnetism. In the former case, the periodical changes are to be regarded as the effect only of the *variations* of that influence; in the latter, they must be considered as its entire result, the action in this case only serving to modify the phenomena due to some more potent cause. It may be fairly hoped that a diligent study of this class of phenomena will not only illustrate this and other doubtful points in the physical foundation of the science; but also, whenever that physical cause shall come to be fully known, and be made the basis of a mathematical theory, the results obtained will serve to give to the latter a numerical expression, and to test its truth. Even the knowledge of the empirical laws of the hourly and monthly fluctuations must prove a considerable accession to science; and (as one of its more obvious applications) will enable the observer to reduce his results, as far as this class of changes is concerned, to their *mean* values.

For the complete determination of the hourly and monthly changes of the magnetic elements, a persevering and laborious system of observation is requisite. The *irregular* changes are so frequent, and often so considerable, as (partially at least) to mask the regular; and the observations must be long continued at the same hours, before we can be assured that the irregularities do not sensibly affect the mean results. Again, in a theoretical point of view, the nocturnal branch of the curves by which the periodical changes are represented is quite as important as the diurnal; and it is manifest that nothing can be done towards its determination without the co-operation of a number of observers. At each of the observatories about to be founded by the Her Majesty's Government and by the East India Company, there will be three assistant observers placed under the command of the director; and it is intended that the observations shall be taken *every two hours* throughout the twenty-four. In order that this series of observations, which is especially destined for the determination of the periodical changes, may at the same time cast some light upon the irregular movements, it is proposed that they shall be *simultaneous* at all the observatories. The hours which have been agreed upon are the *even* hours (0, 2, 4, 6, &c.) *Göttingen mean time*. It is likewise intended that *one* observation of the twelve shall be a *triple* observation, the position of the magnets being noted according to an arrangement which will be hereafter explained The time of this triple observation will be 2 P.M., Göttingen mean time.

The barometer, and the wet and dry thermometers, will be registered at each of the twelve magnetic hours.

No observation will be taken on Sunday.

No distinct series of observations is required for the determination of the *secular* variations. In the case of the *declination*, the yearly change will be obtained by a comparison of the monthly mean results (for the *same month* and *same hour*) in successive years. The observations of two years only will thus furnish 144 separate results, from which both the periodical and the irregular changes are eliminated; so that great precision may be expected in the final result, notwithstanding the limited period of observation. The same mode of reduction will apply to the two components of the *intensity*, provided that no change shall have taken place in the magnetic moment of the bars employed. In the latter event, recourse must be had to the *absolute* determinations for a knowledge of the secular changes.

The subject of the *irregular* movements has acquired a prominent, and almost absorbing interest, from the recent discoveries of Gauss. It has been ascertained that the resultant direction of the forces, by which the horizontal needle is actuated at a given place, is *incessantly* varying, the oscillations being sometimes small, sometimes very considerable;—that similar fluctuations occur at the most distant parts of the earth's surface, at which corresponding observations have been as yet made;—and that the instant of their occurrence is the same everywhere. The intensity of the horizontal force has been found subject to analogous perturbations.

For the full elucidation of the laws of these most interesting phenomena, it is of the first importance that the stations of observation should be separated as widely as possible over the earth's surface, and that their positions should be chosen near the points of maxima and minima of the magnetic elements. This has been in a great measure accomplished as regards the observatories about to be founded by Her Majesty's Government and by the East India Company. The stations are wide asunder in geographical position, and they are in the neighbourhood of points of prominent interest in referenec to the isodynamic lines. The results of observation at these stations will soon testify whether the shocks to which the magnetic needle is subject, are of a local or of a universal character as regards the globe; and in either event we may expect that they will furnish information of great value (in reference to a physical cause) as to the magnitude of the phenomena in different places, and the elements on which it depends.

In the observations destined to illustrate these phenomena, it is proposed to follow the plan laid down by Gauss, as nearly as the proposed extension of that plan will permit. The Göttingen terms* will be observed as agreed on by the German Magnetic Association; but in place of confining them to four in the year, as at present, they will be extended to every month.

The four *terms* at present agreed upon by the German Magnetic Association occur in the months of February, May, August, and November, and commence on the *Friday preceding the last Saturday* of the month, at 10 P.M. *Gottingen mean time.* It is proposed that the eight additional terms shall be held on the *Wednesday nearest the 21st* of the eight remaining months; the hour of commencement being the same as before.

Thus, in the course of the next three years, there will be thirty-six terms of simultaneous observation. The days of commencement of these terms are given in the subjoined table. The hour of commencement will be, in all cases, 10 P.M. *Gottingen mean time.*

In these terms the declination magnetometer will be observed at intervals of *five minutes*, the corresponding moments of observation being the *full* minutes, 0, 5, 10, 15, &c. Gottingen mean time. Each of the force magnetometers will be observed at intervals of *ten minutes*; the epochs of observation of the horizontal force magnetometer being $2^m 30^s$, $12^m 30^s$, $22^m 30^s$, &c., and those of the vertical force magnetometer $7^m 30^s$, $17^m 30^s$, $27^m 30^s$, &c. Gottingen mean time. By this arrangement an observation will be taken every $2\frac{1}{2}$ minutes, and the observer will have sufficient time between the observations to transfer his attention from one instrument to the next without embarassment or confusion.

---

* For the details of the arrangements of the "*term observations*," see the translation of Gauss's memoir in Taylor's Scientific Memoirs, vol. ii. part v.

Days of commencement of the terms of simultaneous observation, during the years 1840, 1841, and 1842.

Month.	1840.	1841.	1842.
January	Wednesday 22	Wednesday 20	Wednesday 19
February	Friday 28	Friday 26	Friday 25
March	Wednesday 18	Wednesday 24	Wednesday 23
April . ..	Wednesday 22	Wednesday 21	Wednesday 20
May .	Friday 29	Friday 28	Friday 27
June. ..	Wednesday 24	Wednesday 23	Wednesday 22
July	Wednesday 22	Wednesday 21	Wednesday 20
August.	Friday 28	Friday 27	Friday 26
September	Wednesday 23	Wednesday 22	Wednesday 21
October	Wednesday 21	Wednesday 20	Wednesday 19
November	Friday 27	Friday 26	Friday 25
December. ..	Wednesday 23	Wednesday 22	Wednesday 21

The naval expedition is supplied with a similar equipment of instruments to that of the fixed observatories. Should therefore the ships be under the necessity of wintering in the ice,—and generally, on every occasion when the nature of the service may render it necessary to pass a considerable interval of time in any port or anchorage,—the magnetometers should be established, and observations made with all the regularity of one of the fixed observatories, and with strict attention to all the same details.

The selection of proper stations for the erection of the magnetometers, and the extent of time which can be bestowed upon each, must in a great measure depend on circumstances, which can only be appreciated after the Expedition shall have sailed. The observatory at St. Helena (the officers and instruments for which will be landed by Captain Ross,) will in all probability,—and that at the Cape (similarly circumstanced in this respect) may possibly,—be in activity by the time the ships arrive at Kerguelen's Land; which we would recommend as a very interesting station for procuring a complete and as extensive a series of corresponding observations as the necessity of a speedy arrival at Van Diemen's Land for the establishment of the fixed observatory at that point will allow; taking into consideration the possibility of obtaining during the intermediate voyage, a similar series, at some point of the coast discovered by Kemp and Biscoe. In the ulterior prosecution of the voyage, a point of especial interest for the performance of similar observations will be found in New Zealand, which, according to the sketch of the voyage laid before us by Captain Ross, will probably be visited shortly after the establishment of the Van Diemen's Land observatory. The observations there will have especial interest, since, taken in conjunction with those simultaneously making in Van Diemen's Land, they will decide the important question, how far that exact correspondence of the momentary magnetic perturbations which has been observed in Europe, obtains in so remote a region, between places separated by a distance equal to that between the most widely distant European stations.

In the interval between quitting Van Diemen's Land and returning to it again, opportunities will no doubt occur of performing more than one other series of magnetometer observations, the locality of which may be conveniently left to the judgement of Captain Ross, bearing in mind the advantage of observing at stations as remote as possible from both Van Diemen's Land and New Zealand.

The research for the southern magnetic pole and the exploration of the antarctic seas will afford, it may be presumed, many opportunities of instituting on land hitherto unknown, or on firm ice when the vessel may be for a time blockaded, observations of this description; and in the progress of the circumnavigation, the line of coast observed or supposed to exist under the name of Graham's Land, or those of the islands in that vicinity, South Shetland, Sandwich Land, and finally on the homeward voyage the Island of Tristan d'Acunha, will afford stations each of its own particular interest.

The *term* days which occur twelve times in the year, will be especially interesting, as periods of magnetometrical observations by the Expedition, when the circumstances of the voyage will permit. For the determination of the existence and progress of the diurnal oscillation, in so far as that important element can be ascertained in periods of brief duration, it will be necessary to continue the observations hourly during the twenty-four for not less than one complete week. At every station where the magnetometers are observed, the absolute values of the dip, horizontal direction, and intensity will require to be ascertained.

Sydney would be with great propriety selected for a station of absolute measurements, as there can be no doubt of its becoming at no distant period a centre of reference for every species of local determination.

In case of the occurrence of Auroras, the hourly should at once be exchanged for uninterrupted observation, should that not be actually in operation. The affections of the magnetometers during thunderstorms, if any, should be noticed, though it is at present believed that they have no influence.

During an earthquake in Siberia in 1829, the direction of the horizontal needle, carefully watched by M. Erman, was uninfluenced; should a similar opportunity occur, and circumstances permit, it should not be neglected.

Should land or secure ice be found in the neighbourhood of the magnetic pole, every attention will of course be paid to the procuring a complete and extensive series of magnetometric observations, which in such a locality would form one of the most remarkable results of the Expedition.

2. FIGURE OF THE EARTH.

The Expedition being provided with invariable pendulums, with all the necessary apparatus for determining the length of the seconds pendulum, it will be highly desirable to have this important observation made at several points, especially in high southern latitudes, and generally speaking at points as remote as possible from those at which it has already been determined. The selection of these must depend on local circumstances, as regards convenience for landing the instruments and executing the operations, as well as on the times of arrival at the several points.

It would also be desirable, if a convenient opportunity occurs, to swing the pendulums on the top of some high mountain; in which case they should also be swung at the foot of the same mountain, in order to determine the difference produced by the elevation, or other effect of the high land.

Another experiment which it would be desirable to make, is to swing the pendulum on a large field of fixed ice, as far from the land as possible; and likewise on the nearest shore to such position. In all these cases more than one pendulum should be used; and at least three knife edges should be employed, in order to guard against any unforeseen anomaly that may arise.

It is scarcely necessary to state, that the direction of the line or motion, with respect to the magnetic meridian, should be noted at each station.

3. TIDES.

With regard to *tides*, it is not likely that Capt. Ross's other employments will allow him to pursue observations on that subject with any continuity; nor is it desirable that he should do so, excepting he were able to carry on his observations to a much greater extent than is consistent with the nature of the Expedition. There are, however, certain objects which may be answered by occasional and detached observations, which may be briefly stated.

1. At all stations on the coasts visited, and especially at all detached islands in the middle of wide seas, it is desirable to obtain the *correct establishment* of the place, or mean lunitidal interval. This may be done with tolerable accuracy by a few observations of successive high waters; and these must be reduced with a proper allowance for the age of the moon; that is, not only for the time of the moon's transit, but also for the semimenstrual inequality. The things to be observed are, the *mean solar* time of high water, the rise of the tide from low to high water, and, if convenient, the *mean solar* time of low water.

2. It is desirable to ascertain the existence and amount of *the diurnal inequalities* in such situations as have been spoken of. For this purpose the heights of high water should be observed for several successive tides, day and night; and, if possible, this should be done when the moon is at her greatest declination, or a few days later; at any rate, not when the moon is in the equator, nor a few days after that period.

It is very probable that a diurnal inequality of the *heights* will be detected; but it appears not worth while to attempt, under the circumstances, to detect a diurnal inequality of the *times*.

4. Meteorology.

A complete meteorological register will of course be kept in each ship during the whole continuance of the voyage; skeleton forms for the arrangement of the observed and reduced quantities are furnished. These are adapted for intervals of observation of six hours throughout the twenty-four; and although hourly observations be made, as is undoubtedly to be desired, yet the regular entry and reduction of the observations for the hours in the skeleton forms is nevertheless essential, for the sake of future comparison with those similarly entered and reduced at the fixed stations. But in considering the suggestions which it may be proper to offer upon this branch of the subject, the Council have been induced to take a more comprehensive view than might at first be supposed to be called for by the immediate objects of the Expedition. So many references have lately been made to them upon the subject of directions for meteorological observations, that they have embraced the opportunity of proposing a plan of extensive co-operation applicable alike to the Expedition, to the Magnetic Observatories about to be established, and to other Observatories for which directions have been thus solicited. The Council have therefore thought it more convenient to draw up a separate Report, which, as regards the Antarctic Expedition and the Magnetic Observatories, may be considered as supplementary to the present one.

In the way of general remark on this subject it may be observed, that it is impossible to pay too much attention to the zero points of the instruments, especially the barometer. Every thermometer and barometer, furnished both to the ships and for the observatories, will in the first instance have been carefully compared with those of the Royal Society; and one barometer in each ship should be continually referred to as a standard, whenever the instruments are landed and on their return on board, so as to detect and take account of any change which may have occurred in the interval: while the two standards, whenever the ships are in company, will become checks on each other through the medium of the register. Nor should the opportunity be lost of comparing these standard barometers (by the intervention of portable ones) with the standard barometer of the Cape Observatory, and with that used at Port Arthur, Van Diemen's Land, in the meteorological register kept by Sir J. Franklin's orders by Mr. Lempriere, as well as with the standard at the observatory at Paramatta, and with any other instrument likely to be referred to as a standard or employed in research elsewhere.

The general fact that the barometer at the level of the sea does not indicate a mean atmospheric pressure of equal amount in all parts of the earth,—but, on the contrary, that the equatorial pressure is uniformly less in its mean amount than that at and beyond the tropics,—was first noticed by Von Humboldt, and has since been demonstrated by the assemblage of many observations made during voyages and on land by Schouw, as well as by other observations, an account of which will be found in the Reports of the Meteorological Committee of the South African Philosophical Society for 1836 and 1837. This inequality of mean pressure is a meteorological phenomenon of the greatest and most universal influence, as it is, in fact, no other than a *direct measure of the moving force*, by which the great currents of the trade-winds are produced; so that the measure of its amount, and the laws of its geographical distribution, lie at the root of the theory of these winds. The progress of barometric depression on approaching the line, and re-ascension in receding from it, will therefore be watched with interest proportionate to its intrinsic importance during the voyage outwards and homewards.

But it may very well happen that phenomena purely local of the same nature, may exist, not as *cause* but as *effect*; in other words, that the regular currents once established may, in particular localities, determined by the configuration of continents and by the influence of oceanic currents, or other causes, form permanent eddies or atmospheric ripples, so to speak, under which the mean pressure may deviate materially from the general average. An instance of permanent barometric depression of this kind, in the neighbourhood of the sea of Ochotzk, has been supposed by Erman; and a second seems to be pointed out in the neighbourhood of Cape Horn, by some remarks stated to have originated with Captain Foster; and it is not impossible that something of the same kind, but of an inverse character, may be found to obtain in that remarkable district of Siberia mentioned by Erman, where during winter clouds are unknown and snow never falls; and it is somewhat curious to notice that the localities in question are not far from antipodes to each other.

In the outward and homeward passages of the Expedition across the equator (especially should the ships be delayed by calms), opportunity will be presented of determining the amount of diurnal barometric fluctuation, apart from the interfering influence of land and sea breezes, or their equivalents far inland, which in all land observations encumber and disturb this somewhat obscure phenomenon; as well as for ascertaining, also apart from those influences, the existence or non-existence of that difference between the diurnal and nocturnal maxima and minima, which has been proved to exist in some localities, and surmised to be general[*].

Connected with the equatorial barometric depression, and the ascensional current of heated air which produces that depression, is a phenomenon which may serve to elucidate the mechanism of this current in its origin, as well as to illustrate the mode in which ascending currents occasionally produce rain. It cannot be supposed that the whole body of the equatorial atmosphere rises *en masse*, or with any regularity or steadiness. Such a movement would be out of analogy with what we know of the movements of fluids in general.

[*] See Reports of Met. Com. S. A. Phil. Soc. above referred to.

Its *tendency* to rise is general, but this tendency is diverted by a thousand local influences, and concentred on particular points, where it results in ascending columns and sheets, between which wind-flaws, capricious in their direction and intensity, and often amounting to sharp squalls, mark out the course of their feeders and of the indraft of cooler air from a distance to supply their void. Now the existence of such ascending columns is rendered frequently visible in a very unequivocal way, by vast piled-up masses of cloud of that peculiar form which has been called *cumulostratus*, the bottom being flat and ill-defined, the upper parts towering to an immense height, and ragged with great protuberances. From the bases of these great cumular piles are almost constantly seen to descend those violent showers so common in the calm latitudes.

It would be interesting on many accounts to obtain *measures*, even if somewhat vague, of the altitudes at which the *bases* of these clouds rest, as well as of the height of their summits, and to measure the temperature of the rain which falls from them at successive periods, as they pass over the ship, so as to ascertain whether the rain which falls along their axis be not colder (from coming at least in part from a greater elevation) than that from their skirts. The vapour plane, in such circumstances, being nearly or precisely uniform over vast tracts of sea, the altitude of the base of such cloud vertically overhead may be considered the same as that of any other favourably situated for measure. In fact the determination of the *mean height of the vapour plane* at and near the equator is one of high meteorological import, and is connected by no circuitous steps with all the most interesting questions regarding the distribution of aqueous vapour over the globe and the irrigation of the continents.

5. Distribution of Temperature in the Sea and Land.

Connected as this subject is with meteorology, it requires in some points of view to be considered apart. As the currents in the atmosphere are produced by the difference of temperature in its polar and equatorial regions, so it may be contended are those of the ocean by differences of temperature due to the same geographical causes. Such is the view taken by M. Arago in his elaborate instructions for the voyage of the *Bonite*, and it would appear undoubtedly more just than that which attributes them *wholly* to the friction and pressure of the winds. Nevertheless it must not be forgotten that there is an essential difference in the modes of action in the two cases. The sun's heat is effective in heating the air mainly *from below*, where it is in contact with the earth or water which absorb the rays and communicate them to the air above. In the sea the case is otherwise. The sun's rays are totally absorbed at the surface, and no ray reaches the bottom of any sea deserving the name. No deep stratum of water, therefore, can be permanently maintained by the sun's *direct* heat at a temperature greatly above what it would have independently of its direct action. Hence the motive power in a system of currents so originating must be sought, not in the *ascensional* force at the equator, but in a *descensional* one in the polar regions, or rather in that one polar region in which winter prevails. The order of the phenomena then is precisely the reverse of what obtains in the atmosphere; moreover the seat of the efficient agency is not only much less extensive than in the case of the atmospheric currents, but also subject to a semiannual shifting from one to the other extremity of the earth's axis, both which causes must tend greatly to diminish the average energy of the effect.

Practically speaking, the question resolves itself into one of fact, which observation only can decide. Is there in the whole column of water between the surface of the ocean and its bed at the poles, as compared with a column of equal depth at the equator and *in free communication with it*, a descensional power or not? and what is its amount? These questions can only be resolved by observations of the temperature and saltness of the sea, at various and considerable depths, in different latitudes, and under a great variety of local circumstances. The procuring such observations, and the preservation of specimens of the water, or the determination on the spot of their specific gravities, will afford a useful occupation in calms, and may be recommended as well worthy of attention. Theoretically speaking, the subject is more complicated than at first appears, since it cannot but be that some considerable portion of solar heat absorbed by the equatorial continents,—in place of finding its way out of the earth by radiation at the poles, in the mode of subterraneous communication suggested by Fourrier,—must escape through the bed of the ocean into its waters, and so be carried into their circulation.

Opportunities for determining the temperature of the ocean at great depths must of course be rare; but at moderate depths it can always be done with comparatively little trouble, and we would, therefore, suggest the propriety of making observations of this element at two moderate and constant depths (say 150 and 300 fathoms), by the aid of a self-registering thermometer attached to a sounding line whenever the ship's way shall be such as to allow their being made with precision.

6. Currents of the Ocean.

These are either subaqueous or superficial, and, like those in the atmosphere, both may coexist at the same place, with different directions and velocities. Of the former we know almost nothing, and of the latter but little compared with what would be desirable and most useful. The practice of daily throwing overboard a bottle corked and sealed with the latitude and longitude of the ship at noon ought not to be neglected. A single instance of such a record being found may suffice to afford indications of the utmost value, while the trouble and cost are too trifling to mention.

As no sea can be supposed absolutely motionless, the presence of a shoal, by casting up at the surface water which, but for it, would have continued to sweep along at a greatly lower level with the general body of the current, must bring the temperature of the surface water into nearer correspondence with that below. In low latitudes the surface water is hotter than that below; and accordingly it is a general remark, that the temperature sinks as the water shoals, or even in passing over banks whose depth is very considerable. If this theory of the phenomenon be correct, the contrary ought to be observed in situations where the surface water is colder than that below, as it is known to be under particular circumstances in the Polar Seas. In still larger tracts in high latitudes the seas have nearly a uniform temperature throughout their whole depth. In such circumstances should any superficial variation of temperature be observed in passing over a shoal or bank, it could only be ascribed to radiation. The subject is one of considerable interest to the navigator, as the approach to land or to shoal water is indicated by the thermometer with a high degree of sensibility. We have before us recent observations of this kind, the one at entering Table Bay in 1834, the other at quitting it in the present year. In the former case the temperature fell 9° Fahr. in passing from deep water into the Bay; in the latter under reverse circumstances a rise of no less than 13° Fahr. was experienced, the temperature of the air remaining unaltered. The last-mentioned observations being very remarkable, the particulars are annexed.

Memorandum of observations made on board the Earl of Hardwicke, H.E.I.C.S. by Captain Henning.

March 17th, 1839. Temperature of air at 5ʰ P.M., four miles from

Cape Town	64°·0
Of Sea .. .. •	52°·0
5ʰ 30ᵐ One mile north of Robben Island. Air	64°·0
Sea . ... • ..	57°·0
March 18th at sea. Air	64°·0
Sea	65°·0

The opportunity of re-examining this point, and in general, of investigating more closely the phenomena of temperature in the neighbourhood of the Lagullas Bank, will, of course, not be lost sight of as the ships approach to and leave the Cape.

The distribution of temperature over the globe must greatly depend on the intensity which the solar rays possess on attaining the surface of the earth after traversing the atmosphere in different latitudes. To subject this point to direct inquiry in a mode which after many years' trial has been found to give very satisfactory results, Actinometers are provided, and accompanied with very precise directions for their use. They should be observed only when the sky in the immediate neighbourhood of the sun is perfectly free from visible cloud. On the other hand, depression of temperature caused by diurnal and nocturnal radiation by the only means we at present possess for that purpose,—viz. that of thermometers blackened and exposed in reflectors to the sky,—will form a useful and valuable supplement to the actinometric researches. With a view to the collection of facts illustrative of the distribution of temperature on land, wherever the ships may touch with a prospect of remaining some days, no time should be lost, on landing, in burying in the earth one or more bottles (filled with spirits, if there should be danger of water freezing), well packed in cases, or boxes stuffed with non-conducting matter, such as woollen cloth, pounded charcoal, &c., but so as to leave easy access to the neck, which should be wide enough to introduce the bulb and stem of a good thermometer, so as to take the temperature of the contained liquid rapidly, before it can have become altered by exposure in the air on taking up the bottle. Bottles so arranged should be buried at depths of three, six, nine, twelve, &c. feet*, according to the facilities of penetrating the soil, and abandoned till the time of departure, so as to ensure their acquiring the precise temperature of the soil; and when taken up should immediately have the temperature of the included liquids ascertained. In case of very prolonged sojourn, monthly readings should be taken. The temperatures of all springs and wells should also be diligently noted and registered.

Connected with the transcalescence of the air, is the transparency of the sea. The stimulus of the solar light no doubt affects the surface of mollusca at great depths, and numerous points of physical inquiry would be elucidated if we knew the co-efficients of extinction of the solar rays by pure sea water. As far as the luminous rays are concerned (or at least the chemical), the actual intensity of these rays at various depths might be very easily ascertained, both for direct sunshine and that of cloudy daylight, by the aid of Mr. Talbot's sensitive paper; which, duly guarded from wet by varnish and interposition between glass plates, might be sunk, face upwards in a small frame, while a portion of the same paper, cut from the same sheet, should be similarly exposed on deck, and partially shaded, inch by inch, from minute to minute, (or for a smaller interval according to the sensitiveness of the paper) with a view to immediate comparison, between decks by a light not strong enough to alter the tint.

A simple and convenient mode of photometric measurement is also furnished by the sensitive paper above alluded to, by the exposure of a small portion of it to the sun at noon for a given time, suppose ten seconds, and subsequent comparison with a scale of tints. Paper duly prepared for these purposes will be supplied for the use of the expedition. During solar eclipses such paper ought to be exposed at intervals of five minutes.

The temperature of the soil under the direct influence of the sun as indicated by a thermometer barely covered with dry earth, is an element of importance to the botanist, and may be recommended as an apt accompaniment to actinometric observations. The thermometer used should have a scale reading at least to 180° Fahr.

The height of the line of perpetual snow, by whatever indications marked, should also be ascertained, wherever practicable.

7. DEPTH OF THE SEA.

Soundings to as great a depth as practicable should be taken wherever opportunities may offer. Great difficulty, however, is well known to exist in the way of procuring any exact result, or indeed

* These are the depths adopted in Mr. Forbes's recent experiments.

any result at all in very deep seas; and various methods (all objectionable) have been proposed and tried. Could any means be provided to keep out the water from a shell, and at the same time ensure its explosion on striking the bottom, the time elapsed, between casting the shell overboard and hearing the explosion, would indicate the depth with great precision; nor need we fear that, if the explosion took place, the sound would not be heard, sound being propagated through water with infinitely greater sharpness and clearness than through air. To overcome the enormous external pressure, and to enable the charge to burst the shell, it is probable that mere gunpowder might not suffice. Should this be apprehended, a mixture of fulminating mercury with the charge in about equal proportions, would probably effect the object. At least we know, from experience, the vast increase of bursting power which is communicated to powder by such addition. It has also been suggested that an *echo* from the bed of the ocean might be heard, were a shell exploded just beneath the surface (as an echo from the earth is heard in the car of a balloon); and attempts, though imperfect ones, have been made to subject this proposal to trial, the reason of the failure of which does not very distinctly appear. The maximum depth of the sea is a geological datum of such value, that a few failures incurred in attempts may very well be tolerated when placed in competition with the interest of even partial success.

8. Atmospherical Phenomena.

There can be little need to call the attention of navigators to anything relating to winds, storms, lightning, &c.; yet there are some points to which attention may be expressly drawn, viz. to such distribution and movements of the clouds as indicate the existence at the same time of an upper and an under current of wind moving in opposed or differing directions. In such cases, the sun, moon, or a star should be taken as a point to fix the eye. In storms the barometer should be very assiduously noted in relation to the varying phases of the gale and the changes of wind, and particularly to those sudden shifts of wind which characterize revolving storms. The Council are not aware that the state of the barometer during "a white squall" has ever been very carefully noted from instant to instant; or that it, or the more sensitive sympiesometer, have been referred to during the approach and recess of a waterspout.

The phenomena of ordinary thunder-storms may be thought to afford little matter for remark, and extraordinary ones will be noted of course. Yet there is one point to which we should wish that some attention might be paid,—it is the sudden gush of rain which is almost sure to succeed a violent detonation immediately over-head. Is this rain a *cause* or a *consequence* of the electric discharge? Opinion would seem to lean to the latter side, or rather, we are not aware that the former has been maintained or even suggested. Yet it is very defensible. In the sudden agglomeration of many minute and feebly electrified globules into one rain drop, the quantity of electricity is increased in a greater proportion than the surface over which (according to the laws of electric distribution) it is spread. Its tension therefore is increased, and may attain the point when it is capable of separating from the *drop* to seek the surface of the *cloud*, or of the newly-formed descending body of rain, which, under such circumstances, and with respect to electricity of such a tension, may be regarded as a conducting medium. Arrived at this surface, the tension for the same reason becomes enormous, and a flash escapes.

The following points should be observed, with a view to this mode of regarding the formation of lightning. 1st. The actual electric state of *that* rain which follows suddenly after a discharge originating vertically over head.

2nd. Does lightning ever happen without rain *in the immediate point where it originates*, or at least without a rapid formation and increase of cloud at that point?

3rd. Does it ever lighten from a cloud undergoing actual diminution from evaporation?

4th. Do the cumular clouds, already noticed as continually forming and raining in the calm latitudes, usually or frequently send forth flashes of lightning; and if so, under what conditions, and with what effects?

Observations of Aurora will form a highly interesting subject, should the Expedition be under the necessity of wintering, or of passing any of the later part of the season in south latitudes admitting of their exhibition. Their effects on the magnetic needle will of course be narrowly watched; but all their phenomena should be minutely registered, such as the formation, colour, extent, situation, movement, and disappearance of arches, patches, banks, and streamers. In particular we would draw attention to an appearance which sometimes occurs, and which cannot but be regarded as highly instructive. It consists in *pulsations* propagated with more or less swiftness through *patches* of sky *of definite forms*, which however become visible only in successive portions, as the pulse traverses them, giving the idea of masses of vaporous matter not visible *per se*, but rendered fitfully so, either by a band of light cast in succession over every part of them from without, or by a temporary phosphorescence developed within their substance when traversed by electric matter. Such pulsations as above described formed very remarkable features of the auroras of October 12, 1833, and of January 18, 1839.

Any indication of the *near vicinity* of auroral phenomena, or of their existence at a level below that of ordinary clouds, should be most minutely investigated at the moment, and carefully and circumstantially recorded.

On the nights from the 11th to the 14th of November the sky should be watched for the periodical meteors, whose existence seems now to be placed out of doubt; as also from the 9th to the 13th of August; and in general any remarkable display of shooting stars should be noted. The zodiacal light also should be observed in clear nights, with a view to the better defining its limits, and ascertaining if it be really, as some have supposed, variable in its extent

or lustre. Remarkable halos, parhelia, and other atmospheric phenomena, should be recorded, and careful measures of their dimensions taken with sextants or other instruments.

9. Variable Stars.

During night-watches in clear weather, in southern regions, many
interesting observations might undoubtedly be made by any one ac-
quainted with the constellations, or provided with a celestial map,
as to the comparative lustre and variability of stars. Especially we
would point out to the attention of such an observer the stars α Hy-
dræ et Crateri as certainly, and δ Orionis as probably, variable; the
former at its greatest brightness being equal to ε Argûs, and at its
least equal or somewhat inferior to δ Argûs, which are the best stars
for comparison with it. Its period of change, however, being only very
imperfectly known, additional observations would be valuable. The
remarkable star η Argûs should also be compared with others of the
same apparent brightness, or nearly so, with a view to continue the
history of its late extraordinary change of lustre. And we would
earnestly recommend to any one who may undertake such observations, to form a list of a certain moderate number of stars, graduating
from the first magnitude downwards by almost insensible steps, and
having rendered himself familiar with them, to note their arrangement in order of brightness,—not once only, but on a great many
nights, forming on each occasion separate independent judgements;
trusting on no account to any printed catalogue, and diligently recording and preserving his memoranda. Such observations are not
part of the ordinary business of astronomical observatories, and are
therefore neglected and abandoned to the amateur, the traveller, or
the seaman in his night-watches, which they will be found to beguile
of much of their tedium, and to reward by the frequent detection of
variable stars not previously recognized as such.

10. Refraction.

The determination of refractions near the horizon, both of celestial and terrestrial objects in high southern latitudes, will form a
very interesting subject of study. They may be pursued in various
modes, of which perhaps the easiest is to note the disappearance of
particular stars behind the horizontal edge of a board, erected at
some considerable distance from a fixed point of observation, and
then to ascertain, with all precision, the altitude of the line of disappearance, accompanying such observation with the height of the
barometer and thermometer. Vertical diameters of the sun or moon,
when very near the horizon, with the corresponding altitudes, will
also be of use, as well as measurements of the distances of two considerable stars on the same vertical, and direct measures of the altitudes of one and the same star in the progress of its diurnal course
when near the horizon. The curve of terrestrial refraction might
also be actually traced out by a leveling-staff. Any cases of un-

E

usual refraction, mirage, reduplication and inversion of images, and of lateral refraction, should be recorded.

11. Eclipses.

In annular or total solar eclipses the optical circumstances attending the formation and rupture of the ring should be minutely attended to, as well as the defalcation of light and heat, to be measured by their appropriate methods, as detailed in the Meteorological instructions.

The solar eclipses of $\begin{cases} \text{January 11, 1842,} \\ \text{June} \quad \text{27, 1843,} \end{cases}$
may possibly be central, or very large in some part of the progress of the Expedition. In lunar *total eclipses* the occultations of stars, whether large or small, should be looked for, and any apparent projection on the disk noticed. Great attention should also be paid to the intensity, colour, and distribution of illumination over the disk during the *total* eclipse, as indicative of the general state of *the earth's* atmosphere in that great circle of the globe which at the moment is at right angles to the visual ray.

Section II.—GEOLOGY AND MINERALOGY.

The primary object of the expedition being Magnetical Research, —and the officers by whom Geological information is to be collected having various other and important duties to discharge, it is not so necessary to enter into detail with respect to inquiries in Geology and Mineralogy as if the expedition had been intended for more general purposes, with the probability of more time being at its disposal for these inquiries than its immediate objects will allow. A reference to published instructions for collecting and preserving specimens of minerals and fossils;—the indication of some general phenomena which may be deserving of attention in the Antarctic regions;—and the suggestion of some points of inquiry connected with the places at which the ships are expected to touch, will comprise all that need here be stated.

Collection of Specimens.—Under this head full directions are detailed in several publications, most of which are already in possession of Captain Ross or of his officers*.

* 1. Instructions for the collection of Geological Specimens, printed and circulated by the Geological Society, 1830. 2. Instructions for the same object, distributed by Professor Buckland. 3. Directions for collecting Geological Specimens, by Dr. Fitton, subjoined to Captain P. P. King's Voyages on the coast of Australia. The Council would suggest, as also deserving of attentive perusal, the concluding pages in Mr. Darwin's Journal of his Voyage in the Beagle; and M. Cordier's Geological Instructions for the voyage round the world of *l'Astrolabe and La Zélée*; (*Comptes Rendus*, July to December 1837, p. 150 to 155) and for the voyage round the world of the *La Bonite*; (*Comptes Rendus*, Aug. to Dec. 1835, p. 370 to 373)—with those of Mons. Elie de Beaumont, for the Geologists

1. MISCELLANEOUS SUGGESTIONS.

In the present state of science, a collection of mere rock specimens, even of countries the most distant from Europe, will contribute little to our knowledge if made by persons who have but a slight acquaintance with geology. Such persons would do better to confine their chief attention to the procuring of specimens containing organic remains, such as fossil shells, corals, teeth and bones of fishes, and other animals, and impressions of plants. These should be collected, when opportunity offers, in great abundance, every variety of form being sought for; at the same time that numerous individuals of the same species should be obtained.

When the strata appear to belong to the more modern or Tertiary periods, and contain imbedded shells or corals, collect from the sea-shore, and from the bed of the neighbouring sea by means of the dredge, specimens of recent shells and corals, that they may be compared with the fossil species of the same region.

Notice the prevailing species, or those represented by the greatest number of individuals on the beach, or in dredging in the sea, especially in the high southern latitudes.

Make collections of shells in all sheets of water partially connected with the sea, in order to observe any degree of variation in either the fresh-water or marine species, or the intermixture of species.

Observe carefully the *position* of fossils in the beds which afford them. If corals, whether vertical or inclined?

Notice whether testacea are carried up to the cliffs by birds; the quantity of shells thus accumulated, and the state of preservation.

Make especial search for the bones of mammalia in fresh-water deposits, or in those marine strata in which some land and fresh-water shells are intermixed. Seek for and preserve every fragment of fossil bone, especially teeth, or parts of the cranium, and articulating surfaces of the bones of the extremities.

Examine the materials forming the bottom of caves, for bones.

Whenever coal is found, search for impressions of plants and stems of trees: very few coal plants have been brought from any part of

who accompanied the French Expedition to the North of Europe, 1838; (*Comptes Rendus,* Jan. to June)—of which a translation has been published in Jameson's Edinburgh New Philosophical Journal for 1838, Vol. xxv. p. 292 to 317. The last of these papers contains much information respecting the Northern Regions, which well deserves comparison with the Antarctic Phenomena.

In addition to the collection of Voyages which will of course be taken out, the Council would suggest, as connected with Mineralogy and Geology,—Cleveland's Mineralogy; De la Beche's Geological Manual, 3rd edition; Professor Phillips's Geology, 2 vols. 12mo, 1838; De la Beche's volume entitled "How to observe;" Lyell's Elements of Geology; Boué's *Guide du Géologue Voyageur,* 12mo, 2 vols.; Darwin's Journal, &c., in the Beagle; Scoreby's publications on the Arctic Regions; Macculloch's Classification of Rocks; Bakewell's Geology, 5th edition; Lyell's Principles of Geology, 5th edition; Daubeney on Volcanoes, 8vo; the French translation of Van Buch's description of the Canary Islands, 4to, with a folio of plates.

E 2

the southern hemisphere, but they have been found in high northern latitudes.

In any country where the wild aboriginals eat portions of earth during a great scarcity of food, bring specimens for microscopic observation, as these substances often contain the remains of infusorial animals.

Coral reefs.—In sounding from the edge of a reef, at what depth do the massive kinds of coral form the entire surface, and at what depth do they altogether cease to exist? This can be discovered without much difficulty, and attending to the impressions on the arming of a bell-shaped lead. Record all facts, of the depth at which smaller corals can exist; the specimens must be preserved or their genera carefully recorded.

Describe in every case whether a coral reef includes a lagoon, its depth and inclination of sides. If the reef surround land, is there a channel between it and the shore? what is the depth and breadth of this channel, and inclination of the shores? Consider how far the structure of coral reefs is in accordance with Mr. Darwin's theory that the reefs owe their peculiar configuration to the continual growth of the living coral, during the gradual subsidence of the bottom of the sea. (See Darwin's Journal, Chap. XXII. Consult also Capt. Beedy's Voyage to the Pacific, and Lieut. Nelson, Geol. Trans., 2nd Series, Vol. V. p. 103.)

Carefully describe the structure of elevated masses of coral; can they divide into strata? Do they consist chiefly of masses of coral or of hardened sediment? Do the corals retain a vertical position, or are they rounded and waterworn? Is the coral-limestone crystalline? Bring specimens of all species of coral, to ascertain whether the mass of rock be certainly post-tertiary.

How far south do recent corals or reefs occur?

Floating or drift wood and plants.—Record the distance from land, the latitude and longitude at which they are observed; their state of preservation; the position of the trees, if upright; if with their foliage or fruit.

Signs of disturbance and of elevation and depression of land.—Observe the inclination, curvature, and fracture of strata, and whether the strata have been shifted on the opposite side of fissures, and the direction of the fissures with regard to the compass. If more than one set of fissures, note the direction of each set.

Endeavour to ascertain whether the lines or ridges produced by the movement of strata are continued to any great extent; and, if more than one such ridge be found, whether they are parallel.

In all islands, seek for traces of gravel and sea beach, at points above the present level of the sea. Measure, or estimate, the level of such places.

Conflicting statements having been made respecting the reality of a permanent upheaval of the coast of Chili after the earthquake of

1822, and several subsequent convulsions, seek for evidence on this question.

Notice carefully all indications of subsidence of land;—as of the tide reaching deserted houses, or other human works partially or wholly exposed at low water. Whether beds of peat, or stumps of trees, are exposed during any state of the tide, or can be seen constantly covered with water. In making these observations, attend particularly to the outline of the coast; and state whether these indications occur in estuaries, bays, or along straight, open shores, free from sand-banks.

Structure and forms of land.—Record all indications of terraces, in valleys or along sea coasts; the extent to which they may be traced; whether horizontal or inclined,—uninterrupted, or only traceable at intervals. If more than one line of terrace occurs in the same valley or cliff, determine or estimate their elevation above the sea, and the vertical distance between each terrace; examine the materials of which they consist, whether of shingle, sand, or clay; whether they contain any remains of testacea, and if so, whether the shells are of marine or fresh-water species.

Observe whether the sea is deep where there is a bold or precipitous coast, and shallow where the coast is flat, or where exceptions to this rule occur.

Attend, on all occasions, to the gradual or sudden deepening of the sea; also to the soundings of previous navigators, and note if there be at present any difference.

In making soundings in a line transverse to the direction of the coast, observe whether the pebbles at the bottom become smaller and the sand finer on receding from the shore, and at what rate. Note also the forms as well as coarseness of the materials, as such facts throw light on the transporting power of waves and currents.

Make profiles of the soundings, and mark on them whatever the lead may bring up; if living shells, note on the label of the specimen the depth, nature of the bottom, latitude and longitude, distance from the nearest coast, &c.

If an opportunity offers of studying alluvial deposits, mark whether the beds of detritus are horizontal or inclined; if accumulated against abrupt cliffs; the manner in which the materials are disposed, whether horizontally or in sloping beds.

Obtain all the information possible respecting the increase of sand-banks, or the destruction of cliffs and islands by waves and currents.

It will be desirable, M. Cordier remarks, (*Comptes Rendus*, 1835, pp. 371, 372.), whenever an expedition is stationary, to make a minute examination of one or more hills or mountains considered as characteristic of the region where they occur. With this view, specimens of the rocks and fossils should be taken from *all*, or a great number of the beds, from the bottom to the summit, with exact notes of their thickness; and a sketch or section should be made, marked with numbers corresponding to the place of the specimens respectively.

Cleavage.—If planes of cleavage distinguishable from those of stratification are recognised, observe whether the direction of these planes are uniform over large areas; whether they are parallel to ridges and mountain chains; their angle of inclination both relatively to the horizon and to the planes of stratification; their connexion with large fissures, metallic veins or trap dikes, A paper by Professor Sedgwick in Geol. Trans. 2d Series, Vol. III.. ought to be consulted upon this subject. Attend particularly to the cleavage of slate rocks in the southern hemisphere; and the direction of the cleavage planes has been found to be singularly uniform in Terra del Fuego.

Floating masses of ice.—Note their position with respect to latitude and longitude, and the stony or earthy materials which may be found upon or within them.

On the shores of islands, or on coasts much exposed to the action of floating icebergs, observe what effect is produced on the surface of the rocks by their friction.

In rivers or torrents with rocky beds, what effect is produced by the masses of ice borne down by floods on the rocks at the bottom. (See Darwin's Journal, &c., in the Beagle, Addenda, p. 616, and Agassiz, Edin. New Phil. Journal, Vol. XXIII. p. 364.)

Is there reason to believe that icebergs, when running aground, stir up and disturb the sediment, or otherwise affect the bottom?

Are they capable of pushing before them, and pushing up bodily, large masses of sand and shingle, and of disturbing without obliterating the stratification of these masses?

2. Erratic Blocks.

This name has been given to masses of rock often found loose upon the surface, which commonly differ from the stone of the country, and are sometimes very distant from rock masses like themselves. Measure their height, length and breadth. Take specimens of them; note their form, whether irregular and angular, smooth, or polished; their composition, whether like any known masses seen elsewhere. Do they exfoliate on weathering, or by the action of frost? If different from that of the rocks in the adjacent country; whether the rocks on which they rest are furrowed; if most numerous on the summits of ridges, or in valleys; if arranged in any order; if more numerous in one part of a ridge or valley than in others. At what height do they occur above the level of the sea, and at what distance from the shore?

Great erratic blocks are said to occur on the shores of the New Shetland Islands, consisting of granite, which is not found to compose the adjacent rocks.—See Cordier's Instructions.—(*Comptes Rendus*, 1837. pages 152–154.)

See the Account of an American Expedition of Discovery to the South Polar Regions in 1830.

For an account of the blocks in the glaciers of *Spitzbergen*, see De Beaumont's Instructions.—(*Comptes Rendus*, 1838, p. 22.)

3. Volcanic Phenomena.

Record all indications of recent volcanic character; jets of smoke; of flame by night.

If vapours issue from the earth, observe their effects on the adjacent rocks, and procure specimens of the altered and unaltered stone; note the distance to which the change extends.

Where volcanoes are actually in eruption, record accurately the date and duration of their paroxysms; and, when the intensity varies, note the time of the greatest violence, and *contra*.

Ascertain whether Neptunian substances are to be met with amid the detritus of volcanic islands; and to what height sea-shells or other marine remains can be traced.

Among the ejected masses, both of active and extinct volcanoes, many crystalline minerals may be expected. The masses should be broken, and closely examined with a view to their discovery.

All the lavas of existing currents,—volcanic glass, obsidian, pumice, &c., should be carefully observed, collected, and examined for crystals.

Phenomena indicating former earthquakes should be carefully inquired after, and noted; and, in inhabited countries, an attempt should be made to ascertain the traditions on this point.

If dykes of lava, or of trap, traverse other rocks, ascertain whether any changes have been produced in the latter. Obtain specimens of the dykes, and of the altered and unaltered rocks

If the structure of the volcanic mass is exposed in chasms or ravines, observe carefully the dip and direction of the beds. Do the streams of lava and beds of tuff dip away on all sides from a central axis?

Mineral springs, hot springs.—Note their occurrence, the rocks from which they issue, and obtain a large bottle of the water; also specimens of the sediment deposited by them. Record their temperature; the volume of water thrown out; whether they are uniform, or intermittent; whether gas be disengaged from them.

4. Heads of Inquiry at Specific Places.

Cape de Verd Islands, St. Jago.—There is a calcareous stratum near Porto Praya, containing fossil shells, which appear to be all of recent species; a full collection of these would be highly desirable. This stratum extends, in a nearly horizontal line, for several miles on each side of the port. To ascertain the limits of the stratum and its general horizontality at distant parts of the coast would be very interesting, as affording proof of an equable elevation of a volcanic island of not large dimensions. Some square-topped hills at the distance of a few miles from the coast, belong to a more ancient period than the volcanic rocks of the shore; their stratification and form indicate that they form part of a grand circle, which would come under the class of the so-called "craters of elevation." If the geologist has opportunities of visiting places distant from the vessel, the relation of these hills to the general structure of the island will be highly deserving of his attention.

St. Paul's Rock.—Compare this place with Mr. Darwin's description.—(Journal, pp. 7, 8.)

St. Helena.—The beds of mould, which contain abundant land-shells, on the flanks of Flagstaff-hill, are deserving of close attention, as probably several species, and perhaps even bones of birds, may be discovered in them.

Mauritius.—It has been the opinion of several naturalists who have visited Port Louis, that the mountains in that neighbourhood form part of an enormous "crater of elevation." The examination of the stratification of the hills (Mount Bamboo) on the western and southern sides would decide this question, and would afford probably some most curious results. If the geologist can ascertain in what part of the island the bed was discovered, which contained the bones of a land tortoise (a collection of which would for several reasons be very interesting),—and of the Dodo, he will of course carefully examine it.

Isle of Bourbon.—In an old French book of travels, (" *Voyage par un Officier du Roi*") it is said that there are appearances in the land here, which indicate that the sea formerly occupied a higher level.

Kerguelen's Land, and neighbouring islets.—Geology wholly unknown. Do there exist any proofs of the recent elevation of this land ? The presence of erratic boulders should be carefully sought for; also of the " *Moraines* " of Glaciers, or any appearances indicating a lower descent of glaciers in former periods than at present. It is doubtful whether glaciers descend to the sea-coast of the island during winter,—a point which it is highly desirable to determine.

The Entire Fauna, although probably exceedingly limited, of these islands—situated between Africa and Australia, and so far distant from other land, is well worthy of the greatest attention, as serving to throw light on the geographical limits of certain forms.

In Cook's third voyage (4to, vol. i. p. 51 to 90), a copy of which will be in the ships, a map of some detail is given of the north-eastern coast of Kerguelen's Land; with a plate exhibiting three views of the land near Arched Point, and two more distant views which include an extensive range of mountains. In the former of these views it will be perceived that some of the land near Arched Point is arranged in terraces, apparently consisting of strata nearly horizontal, with almost vertical cliffs on escarpments. The more distant views and the map show, that some of the mountains are lofty, and disposed in one or more ranges. Observations relating to these mountains; their heights above the sea; an account of their general structure, composition, the direction, inclination and cleavage of the strata,—with a full collection of specimens, and views and sectional sketches of the coast, will be of the highest interest. As the expedition will probably remain at Kerguelen's Land for several days, an opportunity will be afforded of reaching the interior as well as the mountains near the coast, and of obtaining an extensive collection of the rocks, and, probably, of ascertaining several points of structure. In a more recent map, by the Captain of a South Sea whaler, dated in 1799, (now in the Hydrographer's Office,) it is stated that some of the mountains are covered with perpetual snow. If this be so, the determination of the height of the snow line will be of great value.

Van Diemen's Land.—The prevailing strata near Hobart Town contain shells resembling those of our carboniferous series; a full collection of these, especially from some distant part of the island (as the formation extends to the northern shores), would be very interesting. About a mile north of Hobart Town there is one small quarry of travertine limestone (burnt for lime), which contains the leaves of plants not now found in that country; it is said that shells (and bones?) have, though rarely, been found in it: these, especially any bones, and the leaves, are deserving of careful collection. On the shores of Storm Bay there are obscure appearances of a raised beach. Some miles east of Hobart Town there is said to be a great accumulation of oyster shells, which have been quarried for lime. Ascertain if all these shells are of recent species. In the northern parts of the island large caverns are said to exist in the limestone formation: the great probability of their containing fossil remains need scarcely be alluded to; and if any be discovered, their high interest as compared with the extraordinary fossils brought by Sir Thomas Mitchell from Australia, is certain. No coal plants have yet been sent from the coal strata of Van Diemen's Land.

New Zealand.—On the banks of the valley of the Thames river parallel terraces are said to occur: inquire into their origin. On several parts of the coast there are large accumulations of sea-shells; inquire if all these were brought thither by the natives, or if they indicate a change of level.—Inquire if New Zealand was always as barren of terrestrial mammalia as at present.—The modern tertiary deposits which are said to exist on the coast should be most carefully examined.

Staten Island.—Captain Foster remarked, that at the northwestern extremity of the mouth or entrance of North Port Hatchett there are extensive beds of *graphite*, or black lead, of a good and fine quality; and that the roofs of the large caves are composed almost entirely of this substance. It would be very desirable to obtain specimens.

South Shetland Isles.—At Deception island, it is said, volcanic ashes have been observed alternating with ice.

Ascertain whether there are in any parts of the shores of the Antarctic regions, cliffs of mud and gravel, permanently frozen, for a few feet below the surface, such as are found on the shores of the Arctic sea.—[See Dr. Buckland's Geological Appendix to Captain Beechy's Voyage.]

The acquisition of fossils, whether animal or vegetable, in high southern latitudes, is of the highest importance to geology.

Icebergs.—Compare, generally, the phenomena of Icebergs and Glaciers in the antarctic regions, with the accounts given of those in the north.—See on this subject the works of Scoresby; also De Beaumont's instructions.—(*Comptes Rendus*, 1838, p. 21.)

Section III.—BOTANY AND VEGETABLE PHYSIOLOGY.

The duty of the Botanist should be, to collect specimens and preserve evidence concerning every department of Botany and Vegetable Physiology, not merely in illustration of these subjects as branches of science, but with reference to purposes of general utility.

The vegetation of the Antarctic regions and of the most southern countries which the expedition may visit, should be an object of especial attention, for however sterile and uninviting a place may appear to be, it is most desirable to know exactly what plants those regions produce. Here, therefore, and at all other places, as complete an herbarium as possible should be formed. At Kerguelen's Land, of which the Flora is so little known, this is especially necessary: even at St. Helena, the Cape of Good Hope, and Hobart Town, carefully as the botany of these places has been examined, a dried collection of plants should be made, especially of the lower orders of phænogamous vegetation and of aquatic and submersed plants, whether of fresh or salt water. Fungi also, and Rhizanths, should be diligently sought for, and all those minute species of cryptogamic plants which are parasites.

Though but little accession to our knowledge of Systematic Botany can be anticipated at any of the principal stations of the expedition, many new and interesting facts may be collected in Physiological Botany, if anomalous forms of vegetation be examined, as concerning these so little that is positive has as yet been ascertained in foreign countries. Collections should be made of the stems of Casuarinas, Urticaceous trees, and of twining woody plants, the internal structure of which is frequently at variance with the ordinary plan of vegetable formation. Diligent search should also be made for cases of the occurrence of the embryo buds of Dutrochet. It is probable that attention skilfully directed to these last productions will throw light upon some of the most obscure points of Vegetable Physiology. Most of the specimens of this kind may be preserved in a dry state; but as some will require to be kept moist, it is requisite, for this purpose, that the Botanist should be supplied with bottles, jars, acetic acid and spirit.

Attention should be especially directed to the distribution of remarkable species in each country, regard being paid, in particular, to the elevations at which they are found, and the soils which they seem to prefer, where preference is observable. Connected with this topic are the limits to which cultivated plants extend, and the circumstances under which they succeed or fail. In noting points of this nature, facts concerning the commoner species will be interesting, because they are so frequently neglected, and because of the evidence as to climate which they may be expected to afford. In the absence of this kind of knowledge, it is difficult for persons here to judge correctly respecting the kind of plants it may be desirable to introduce into another country. Should the causes of failure or of success in the cultivation of particular plants be apparent, they ought to be noted down. As an instance of the importance of this branch of inquiry, the Vine at the Cape of Good Hope may be mentioned : the bad quality of Cape wine, with the exception of that produced at the farm of Constantia, is well known : can any physical cause be assigned for this circumstance ? If exotic plants are commonly cultivated with apparent success, they should receive particular notice ; European Oaks, for example, are common about Cape Town, where they are planted for their shade ; the species to which they belong, and the effect of that climate upon their growth, and the quality of their timber, are points deserving of attention.

The original Flora of St. Helena should be fully investigated and carefully distinguished from that which has been gradually formed there by the introduction of numerous plants from various countries. The association of plants in this island will be found extremely curious, and the circumstances which enable species of very different habits to flourish equally well in the same place, notwithstanding their constitutional diversity, are deserving of particular attention. A very detailed catalogue should be formed of these exotics, the degree in which they are affected by their new country should be observed, and an attempt be made to discover the causes which are favourable to the maintenance of so singularly mixed a vegetation in so small an island. Such a catalogue, if well prepared, may be expected to illustrate many difficult and important questions which are connected with the relation borne by vegetation to climate.

Both at St. Helena and Hobart Town, Tree Ferns will be found : those in the former place have the stems destitute of external fibres except near the ground, while the Tree Ferns of Hobart Town are thickly covered with similar fibres from the very summit. The origin of these fibres and the circumstances under which they are produced, are unknown, and should, if possible, be determined; indeed, the, manner of growth of these plants in all other particulars is an interesting subject for careful investigation, as are also the circumstances under which this tropical form of vegetation is produced upon Mount Wellington. In the event of the expedition visiting the southern part of New Zealand, it should also be ascertained under what conditions the Tree Ferns that exist there extend so far beyond the usual geographical limits of such trees, and also whether they are not accompanied by other forms of an equally tropical character.

The northern coast of Van Diemen's Land being in many respects clothed with a different vegetation from the south side, it is desirable to notice the peculiarities of each. At Emu Bay, there exists the *Gunnia australis*, an orchidaceous epiphyte, which is far to the southward of the general range of plants of that kind. It will probably be found that this apparent exception to general rules is dependent upon some local peculiarity of climate. Possibly other species with similar habits occur on the same line of coast; they should be sought for, and particular attention should be paid to the plants with which the orchidaceous epiphytes are associated.

A principal object of inquiry should be, plants yielding useful products of all kinds. It is in this way only that the resources of foreign countries can be ascertained, and it is presumed that in an expedition which will be stationary for considerable periods of time, such inquiries can be easily made. Under the head of useful products the following may be particularly mentioned:

1. *Dietetical, medicinal,* and *poisonous agents* of all kinds. The nature and action of the poisons employed by the natives of many countries are but slightly known.

2. *Dye stuffs.* Attention should be paid, especially to obtain Lichens, as substitutes for the *Roccella tinctoria*, now becoming scarce, and consequently very valuable in European commerce. The fitness of these plants for this purpose may be approximately ascertained by Hellot's lichen test, which is as follows: digest the lichen at a temperature of 130° F. for a few hours, in a weak solution of ammonia, but sufficiently strong to be tolerably pungent. One that is fit for the dyer will yield a rich violet red liquid.

3. *Astringent substances adapted for tanning.* It is desirable to ascertain with accuracy the source of the various astringent extracts imported from New Holland and the neighbouring parts, and which are employed by the tanners of this country.

4. *Fibres adapted for cordage and weaving.* Substitutes for Hemp are very desirable. Great strength, flexibility and freedom from njurious influence in working are three essential qualities of good hemp.

5. Information respecting the source of many of the *ornamental woods* imported from the southern hemisphere is very imperfect. It is desirable, therefore, that inquiries be made on this subject as well as for new kinds of wood.

6. *Gums, resins, volatile oils, fecula.* Especially the source of some resins brought to this country from New Holland, and which are analogous in some properties to the *yellow resin* of that country.

In forming collections of such objects, especial care must be taken when collected to number alike both the products and the plants by which they are furnished, and to note whatever can be learned concerning them, more particularly with regard to their abundance and the facility with which they can be procured. It is also necessary that the observations made by the Botanist himself should be carefully distinguished from such information as he may receive from other persons.

No opportunity is to be lost of collecting information respecting the source and mode of preparation of any vegetable substances known in commerce; for many exotic products, even those with which we are most familiar, have many points connected with their natural history deserving attention.

The vegetation of South Shetland cannot be expected to furnish much that can be made available for purposes of commerce, except Lichens. With respect to these plants, however, it is possible that species fit for the purposes of the dyer may be found in those southern latitudes; and if such should prove to be the case, an additional source of profit may become available for the South-sea traders.

Where the native names of useful plants can be correctly ascertained, they should be preserved; but care must be taken to avoid error in this respect. Implicit credit must not be given to the statements of individual natives; it is only by comparing the separate evidence of different persons, that correctness can be expected.

Collections should be formed of the seeds and bulbs of useful and ornamental plants wherever opportunities occur, and they should be forwarded to Europe from time to time. It is also recommended that duplicate collections be transmitted to the Supreme Government at Calcutta for distribution among the botanical gardens of India. In packing these collections, the best method is to enclose each kind of seed in separate packets of brown paper, which should be placed loosely in canvas bags, or in boxes with holes in their sides, and arrangements should be made for their being transmitted in a cabin, or some well-ventilated part of the ship. Among those seeds which it is more particularly desirable to procure, may be mentioned the arborescent Compositæ of St. Helena, and the native Coniferous plants of all countries, particularly the Phyllocladus or Celery-leaved Pine, and the various species of Athrotaxis inhabiting the mountains of Van Diemen's Land. As the seeds of such plants are apt to suffer from long keeping, and as other instances may occur when it would be desirable to send home young plants instead of seeds, it would be advisable that the expedition should be supplied with one of Mr. Ward's glazed cases, to be used if occasion should arise.

Light is an agent which operates so powerfully upon plants, determining the amount and even nature of their secretions, and influencing in the most essential manner their vital actions, that it would be most interesting to obtain, if possible, some good pho-tometrical observations. The extreme and mean temperatures of the atmosphere, its humidity, the quantity of rain, and the tempera-ture of the earth immediately below and within a few feet of the surface, have also a direct and important bearing upon Vegetable Physiology, especially when considered with respect to the distri-bution of plants, and the arts of cultivation. Observations upon all such points tend to explain the connexion which exists between vegetation and climate, and should be introduced by the Botanist into his report, notwithstanding that they also occur in the Meteoro-logical Journal.

If the observations here recommended be briefly noted in a ta-bular form, and at the time that they are made, the registration of much useful matter which might otherwise escape recollection, will be secured, and a valuable document formed for future reference.

In conclusion, the Council most particularly recommend that the Botanist to the expedition be directed to number all the objects collected by him in one consecutive series; that the dried speci-mens, seeds, woods, and productions of all kinds, shall correspond in number with the plants producing them; and that two complete collections be prepared for Government, of which one shall be for incorporation with the general collections belonging to the public, and the other be preserved separately, to illustrate the botany, &c., of the expedition. The Council also recommend that both these collections be delivered up within six months after the return of the expedition; and, finally, that a report upon the botanical results of the expedition be furnished to Government within six months after its return, every plant or object mentioned in the report bearing the number of the specimens in the collections to be delivered up as above recommended.

Section IV.—ZOOLOGY AND ANIMAL PHY-SIOLOGY.

1. Marine Invertebrata.

THE animals which it is desirable to preserve, and which may first present themselves to the notice of the naturalist in the present ex-pedition, are the floating marine *Mollusca* and *Crustacea*, and those which inhabit the Sargazzo or Gulph-weed.

With respect to the *Mollusca*, all the species of the *Cephalopoda* or Cuttle-fish tribe, and all the *Pteropoda* or lower organized floating Mollusca, should be preserved. If taken alive, they should be allowed to die gradually in sea water, by which means they commonly remain in a relaxed state, and display more of their natural outward form.

When dead, they should be soaked for a short time in fresh water, and then put into spirit; or if transparent, in the saline solution*; to prevent decomposition, which otherwise rapidly takes place.

To each specimen should be attached a number, stamped on sheet tin, corresponding to the entry-number in the Catalogue, in which should be noticed the kind of locomotion, or other vital phenomena, and the colour of the living animal, the latter being speedily altered or lost in the preserving liquor. The larger Crustacea will be liable to become putrid in spirit, unless the soft mass, which fills a large portion of the body, consisting of the liver, &c. be removed. Each specimen of this class, excepting the very minute ones, which will be best preserved in small phials or glass tubes, should be wrapt in a piece of very soft, thin linen or cotton cloth, to prevent the legs from being intermixed or lost, as they are very likely to fall off after having been a short time in spirit.

A very important object of investigation is the development of the Crustacea, from the earliest period at which they can be observed to the perfect state. They may be readily examined even before they leave the egg, by opening the egg under a single microscope. Drawings of these changes are very desirable, and when practicable the eggs and young ones in different stages should be preserved in spirit in short glass tubes. The smaller oceanic Crustacea offer a prolific and hitherto unexplored field of investigation.

Among the floating Mollusca likely to be met with in the tropical latitudes is the *Spirula*, a small Cephalopod with a chambered shell. An entire specimen of this rare Mollusk is a great desideratum; and if it should be captured alive, its movements should be watched in a vessel of sea water, with reference more especially to the power of rising and sinking at will, and the position of the shell during those actions.

The chambered part of the shell should be opened under water, in order to determine if it contain a gas; the nature of this gas should likewise, if possible, be ascertained. As a part of the shell of the *Spirula* projects externally at the posterior part of the animal, this part should be laid open in the living *Spirula*, in order to ascertain how far such mutilation would affect its power of rising or sinking in the water. In the event of a living Pearly Nautilus (*Nautilus Pompilius*) being captured, the same observations and experiments should be made on that species, in which they would be attended with more precision and facility, as the species is much larger than the *Spirula*, and its shell external. The towing-net should be kept overboard at all practicable periods, and drawn up and examined at stated intervals, as some of the rarest marine animals have been taken by thus sweeping the surface of the sea.

A sketch or drawing of Molluscous and Radiate animals, of which

* Common salt.................................... 1 part.
　Alum.. 2 parts.
　Boiling water ....10 parts.
Filter the solution when cold.

the form and colour are liable to be materially altered by death, or when put in spirit, will aid materially in rendering the description of the species useful and intelligible. The *Echinodermata* and *Asterias echinus*, and similar forms, should be soaked in fresh water previously to their being put into spirit.

Care must be taken not to crowd too many soft-bodied Invertebrata in the same bottle, and to change the spirit or preserving liquor at least once, if not oftener.

2. FISHES.

The mode and speed of swimming, living colour, temperature, and any other peculiarity, should be noticed before placing the specimen in spirit.

In very large specimens of the Shark or Ray kind, a section of the jaws, with a part of the vertebral column, should always be preserved as wet preparations, and the remainder of the jaws and vertebral column in a dry state. The eyes, eyelids, and part of the surrounding skin should be preserved in the saline solution. In less bulky specimens the entire head should be taken off by dividing the fish below the heart across the upper part of the liver, by which means the mouths of the oviducts, if it be a female, the heart, gills, and head are all preserved together.

The tail of a Shark may be taken off a little below the anus, and the trunk alone preserved for examination. If the trunk be too large, it should be cut through above the pelvis, and the parts contained in the hinder portion, as the claspers of the male, should be preserved in spirit. If the specimen be a female, separate the two oviducts through their whole length, where they run along the abdomen, on each side of the spine, but keep them attached to the cloaca and its surrounding parts.

If with young, or eggs, take the whole out in the same way without opening the oviducts.

The heads of all fishes should be preserved, when the specimens are too large to be preserved entire.

All external parasites, and those which infest the gills of fishes, should be preserved. The alimentary canal should, in all cases, be examined for the presence of the entozoa, which, if adherent to the coats of the intestine, should be preserved with the part to which they are attached. One of the most interesting fishes of the Southern Seas is the Port Jackson Shark (*Cestracion Philippi*). Moderate-sized specimens of this species should be preserved entire: and the head, vertebræ, with the dorsal spines, viscera, and especially the impregnated oviduct, should be preserved. The Southern Chimæra (*Callorhynchus antarcticus*) merits also the especial attention of the Naturalist, and the same specimens of this species should be preserved as of the Cestracion.

3. REPTILES.

Specimens of Turtle should be carefully examined for parasitic animals; a curious Barnacle (*Chelonobia*) and a Leech (*Hirudo branchiata*) are occasionally found adhering to these marine Reptilia.

In the event of the expedition touching at the Galapagos Islands, specimens of *Amblyrhynchus*, a lizard of marine habits, should be secured, and the particular locality of the capture noted.

4. BIRDS.

The *Chionis* or Sheath-bill of the Falkland Islands and Cape Horn.
The Great Penguin (*Aptenodytes*).
The Penguin of the Isle San Lorenzo.
Of these rare and desirable birds, besides the prepared skins, the entire body should be preserved in spirits for anatomical purposes. The young of the Great Penguin, and the eggs at different stages of incubation, should likewise be similarly preserved.

5. MAMMALIA.

The skulls, skeletons, and viscera of a specimen of each species of the *Cetacea* of the Southern Ocean are worthy of being preserved. With respect to the Sperm Whale, an entire fœtus, or, if of large size, the brain, eyes, pharynx, larynx, and blow-holes, and the viscera; a part of the impregnated uterus; the ovaria, and a portion of the membrane of the fœtus; are all parts worthy of preservation.

The same observations apply to the great Elephant-Seals (*Phoca (Cystophora) proboscidea*); of which the skull and skeleton of both male and female are very desirable.

The skulls or skeletons of all the species of the Southern Seals should be preserved, the sex being noted.

6. IN PARTICULAR REGIONS.

In Australia or Van Diemen's Land the following species are more especially worthy of attention.

Thylacinus Harrisii, Hyæna of the Colonists.

Of this species, the skeletons of male and female, detached skulls, an entire specimen in the saline solution for dissection, the viscera, and more especially the impregnated uterus, and a young specimen for the changes in dentition are particularly desirable; such specimens not having been as yet transmitted to the museums of this country or on the continent.

The skeletons, skulls, and female organs of every marsupial quadruped, and of the *Ornithorhynchus* and *Echidna* (or Porcupine of the Colonists) should be preserved.

The smaller Mammalia of Australia, whether Marsupial or Rodent, should be preserved in spirit, and particular notice taken of their locality and habits.

F

Among the birds of Australia the Lyre-Pheasant (*Menura*) would be an interesting subject for anatomical investigation. Of this species are wanting the skeletons of a male and female, and of the young bird; and the entire body of both sexes in spirit, or the saline solution.

The same with respect to the large-billed Cuckoo (*Scythrops*), and Sea-Partridge (*Glareola*).

In New Zealand similar preparations should be obtained of the *Megapodius*, and of the *Apteryx australis*.

With regard to birds it may be observed, that if spirit be injected down the windpipe, it will pass through almost the whole body by means of the air-cells. In the case of a quadruped preserved in spirit, or in the saline solution, it is proper to inject the preserving liquor into the abdominal cavity and intestinal canal.

Section V.—INSTRUCTIONS FOR MAKING METEOROLOGICAL OBSERVATIONS.

The Council of the Royal Society, while they have been occupied in preparing instructions for making meteorological observations at the fixed magnetic observatories about to be established by the Government at Montreal, St. Helena, the Cape of Good Hope, Van Diemen's Land, and the different stations to be visited by the Antarctic Expedition under Captain James Clark Ross, and in reporting on various references made to them of applications for instructions for similar observations by the Secretary of State for the Colonies, the Honourable Court of Directors of the East India Company, and the Corporation of the Trinity House, have availed themselves of this opportunity for proposing a plan of extensive co-operation, the general adoption of which by observers cannot fail to produce the most advantageous results to meteorological science.

After maturely considering the subject, they do not presume to anticipate that what they may suggest will not be liable to objections, for their object will be to include within their compass many excellent series of observations which are already in progress, rather than to propose a degree of theoretical perfection, the attainment of which the present state of the science may not perhaps admit of. Systematic co-operation is the essential point to which at present every thing else should be sacrificed; and co-operation on almost any plan would most certainly be followed by more beneficial results than any number of independent observations, however perfect they might be in themselves.

The plan of co-operation should, in fact, be regarded at present as merely temporary and preparatory; but if steadily adhered to for a few years, it would certainly furnish the most perfect data for its own correction, which could then from time to time be applied with facility and precision.

The Council are not without hopes that amateurs of science may be induced to conform to these suggestions, even at the temporary sacrifice of their own views and convenience; for no one can reflect on the immense amount of labour which is now rendered useless for want of the requisite uniformity and precision, without being convinced of the necessity of remedying an evil which has already been of too long standing, and continues to be a reproach to science. Many, of course, will not have it in their power to fill up the plan in all its details; but they will contribute greatly to forward the design, if, in such observations as they may find it convenient to make, they strictly comply with the rules proposed. They will be further encouraged to lend their aid to a comprehensive system, by the consideration that it will be adopted by the Government Observatories, as well as by those about to be established by the East India Company, and will of course be acted upon in the comparison and discussion of the observations made at these institutions by the scientific authorities who will be entrusted with the execution of this task.

The suggestions which the Council wish to offer will relate, 1st, to the times of observation; 2ndly, to the situation of the instruments to be observed; 3rdly, to the correction of the observations; 4thly, to a form of registry, which may place many of the results in a striking point of view, and facilitate comparisons.

1. BAROMETERS.

Times of observation.—The purposes of meteorological observations would be most perfectly and most expeditiously obtained by hourly observations throughout the year; but since in the case of private observers in general, and in few public establishments, such a course of unremitting labour cannot be hoped for, it is necessary, for general purposes, to select periods at longer intervals calculated to embrace the extremes of the periodical oscillations to which the pressure of the atmosphere is subject, and to ensure that uniformity of system at different stations on which the value of such observations so much depends. It is probable that the hours of 3 A.M., 9 A.M., 3 P.M., and 9 P.M., nearly coincide with the daily maxima and minima of the barometric column at the level of the sea, over a large portion of the globe; and it is desirable that as extensive a comparison as possible should be instituted at these hours. At the magnetic observatories, it is provided that observations shall be made every second, or even, hour of Gottingen mean time throughout the twenty-four; so that there at least, and in all others which will act in concert and correspondence with them, the complete diurnal cycle will be satisfactorily observed. It would be uselessly super-adding labour, to the already extensive task imposed on these establishments, to require observations also at the hours above recommended for general adoption as *Meteorological* hours. They will, therefore, content themselves with filling up the forms furnished them, as adapted to the meteorological hours, with observations made at the nearest *magnetic* hours to those named at each station.

It is not, however, too much to expect that hourly observations should be made, during 24 hours, once in every month, by those who profess to pursue meteorology in a scientific manner; and when this cannot be effected, it is of the utmost importance that they should be made at least four times in the year, namely, at the summer and winter solstices, and at the spring and autumn equinoxes. One of the results of these hourly observations would probably be the indication of the exact times of the daily maxima and minima of pressure at different stations, which, if not found to coincide with the hours provisionally adopted, might ultimately be substituted for them under future directions. At the magnetic observatories the instruments will be read off hourly, on the days set apart in each month for the *Magnetic Term observations,* and the two-hourly system of observation in all cases continuing uninterrupted, will in effect furnish corresponding observations on all other days, whether arbitrarily chosen to suit private convenience, or in pursuance of the system about to be proposed in the subsequent paragraphs.

Hourly observations at the equinoxes and solstices have been already instituted at numerous points both of Europe and America, as the suggestion of Sir John Herschel, whose directions should be ttrictly attended to. They are as follows:—

The days fixed upon for these observations are the 21st of March, the 21st of June, the 21st of September, and the 21st of December, being those, or immediately adjoining to those, of the equinoxes and solstices in which the solar influence is either stationary or in a state of most rapid variation. *But should any one of those 21st days fall on Sunday, then it will be understood that the observations are to be deferred till the next day, the 22nd.* The observation at each station should commence at 6 o'clock A.M. of the appointed days, and terminate at 6 A.M. of the days following, according to the usual reckoning of time at the place.

The commencement of each hour should be chosen, and every such series of observations accompanied by a notice of the means used to obtain the time, and, when practicable, by some observation of an astronomical nature by which the time can be ascertained within a minute or two.

The Council now propose to extend these observations in regular series to the 21st of every month, with the same reservation with regard to Sundays.

Travellers provided with meteorological instruments who may be stationary on any of these days, may use them with advantage on such opportunities. Such as may ascend high mountains are recommended, *cæteris paribus*, to choose one of these days as affording a greater probability of securing a complete series of corresponding observations than any other; for which reason these observations cannot be too strongly recommended to *residents* in mountainous countries. The geologist, nay even the surveyor, may find his account in traversing his field, barometer in hand, on one of these days, provided he have reason to presume that there exist observers in its neighbourhood who take a part in these observations.

It is to be hoped that to scientific meteorological observers the six-hourly observations may not be found to be impracticable throughout the year; but in any case where it may be impossible to observe regularly at 3 A.M., an effort should be made to include the hour on the days of the new and full moon, and quadratures, or at least on the days of the new and full moon;—as it must be borne in mind, that in what concerns the great meteorological questions on which the most interesting features of the subject depend, the night is quite as important as the day, and has been hitherto far too much neglected.

Whatever hours, however, may be selected for the regular series of observations, the greatest care should be taken not to insert in the register anything deduced by interpolation from observations made at other hours, or anything in short but what has been actually observed,

It is much to be wished that occasional observations may be made under remarkable circumstances, such as during great rises or great falls of the barometer, at the period of great storms, earthquakes, &c.; but such observations should be registered apart.

The barometer should be placed in an apartment subject to as little variation of temperature as possible, and in a good light; and to facilitate night observations, an arrangement should be made for placing behind it a light screened by a sheet of white paper, or other diaphanous substance. Great care should be taken to fix it in a perpendicular position by the plumb-line. Its height must be carefully ascertained above some permanent and easily-recoverable mark, either in the building in which it is situated, or in some more permanent building, or rock, in its immediate vicinity; and no pains should be spared to ascertain the relation which such mark may bear to the level of high and of low water at spring tides, and ultimately to the mean level of the sea.

Changes in the adjustments of meteorological instruments should be most carefully avoided; but whenever any alteration may be absolutely necessary, they should be made with all deliberation, scrupulously noticed in the register, and the exact amount of the change thence arising in the reading of the instrument under re-adjustment ascertained. As far as possible, registers of meteorological observations should be complete; but if, by unavoidable circumstances of absence, or from other causes, blanks occur, no attempts to fill them up by general recollection, or by the apparent course of the numbers before and after, should ever be made.

The observatories established by the Government are furnished with two barometers each, of Newman's construction—the one a standard, and the other portable; and they are accompanied by accurate directions for fixing and observing them.

The standard instrument is of large dimensions, its tube being of the diameter of 0·6 inch. It requires two adjustments: 1st, The whole scale, which is of brass, is moveable, and terminates in an ivory point, which is carefully brought down to the surface of the mercury in the cistern, and the two are known to be accurately in contact when the actual point and its reflexion appear just to touch one another. The scale is laid off from this point from an authentic standard, at the temperature of 32°.

2nd. The second adjustment is that of the vernier, in which the upper part of the scale terminates, to the surface of the mercury in the tube. For this, both the back and front edge are made to coincide, and brought down so as to form a tangent to the curve, and just to exclude the light between them at the point of contact. In making both these adjustments, it is desirable that the eye should be assisted by a magnifying glass. Before the observation is made the instrument should be slightly tapped, to free the mercury from any adhesion to the glass; but any violent oscillation should be avoided.

The portable barometer has only one adjustment, namely, that of the vernier to the upper surface of the mercury in the tube, which adjustment must be effected with the same precaution as in the case of the standard instrument.

This first reading may be entered in the column prepared for it in the register, and beside it the temperature of the mercury carefully read off from the thermometer which dips into the cistern.

As, in the case of the standard barometer, the first measure is taken immediately from the surface of the mercury in the cistern, it requires no correction for the different capacities of the tube and cistern. Neither does it require any correction for capillary action, as the large diameter of the tube renders this correction inappreciable. The portable barometer, however, requires corrections for both these circumstances. For the purpose of the former, the *neutral point* is marked upon each instrument, or that particular height which, in the construction of the instrument, has been actually measured from the surface of the mercury in the cistern.

It is obvious that, in almost every case, the mercury will stand either above or below the neutral point: if above, a portion of the mercury must have left the cistern to enter the tube, and consequently must have lowered the surface in the cistern; if below, a quantity of mercury must have left the tube, and, entering the cistern, raised the level of the mercury in it. For the correction of observations for this circumstance, the relation of the capacities of the tube and cistern have been experimentally ascertained, and are marked upon the instrument: thus, *capacity* $\frac{1}{50}$th, indicates that for every inch of elevation of the mercury in the tube, that in the cistern will be depressed one 50th of an inch. Thus, when the mercury in the tube is above the neutral point, the difference between it and the neutral point is to be divided by the capacity, and the quotient being added to the observed height, the result will be the corrected height. Or if the mercury at the time of observation should be below the neutral point, the difference of the two is to be divided as before, and the quotient to be subtracted from the observed height. Thus, suppose the capacity to be $\frac{1}{50}$th, the neutral point 30 inches, and the observed height 30·500 inches, the difference is 0·5 inch, which divided by 50 gives 0·01 inch to be added to the observed height, producing 30·51, the corrected height; or if the observed height be 29 inches, the difference, 1 inch, divided by 50, gives ·02 inch to be subtracted from the observed height, giving 28·980 inches for the corrected height.

The second correction required is for the capillary action of the tube, the effect of which is constantly to depress the mercury in the tube by a certain quantity inversely proportioned to the diameter of the tube. In the instruments furnished to the fixed observatories the amount has been experimentally determined during their construction, and marked upon the instrument; the quantity is always to be added to the height of the mercurial column, previously corrected as before. For the convenience of those who may have barometers, the capillary action of which has not been so determined, a table of the corrections for tubes of different diameters is placed in the appendix.

The marine barometers furnished to the Antarctic Expedition differ in nothing from the other portable barometers but in the mode of their suspension, and the necessary contraction of the tubes to prevent oscillation from the motion of the ship, and require the same corrections.

When these two corrections have been made in the first reading of the portable barometer, it should agree with the direct observation of the standard barometer; and it is very desirable that frequent comparative observations should be made of the two instruments, in order to ascertain whether there may be any permanent difference between them. Should this be the case, the amount may be marked upon the instrument, and allowed for as an index error, in order that, if an accident should happen to one, the other may be substituted for it without detriment to the regular series of observations.

It is to be presumed that the portable barometer will frequently be employed in ascertaining the altitude of remarkable points in the vicinity of the observatories, or of the more permanent stations of the Expedition.

The instruments furnished to the observatories have been all independently graduated and compared with the standard of the Royal Society; and in all cases it is desirable that such a comparison should be made with some standard instrument of authority, directly, or by means of a good portable barometer. In making such comparisons, all that is necessary is to record five or ten simultaneous readings of both instruments, deliberately made, at intervals of a few minutes from each other, after at least an hour's quiet exposure, side by side, that they may have the same temperature. If compared by two observers, each should read off his own barometer in his usual manner, then each should verify the other's result. By this means the zero of one standard may be transported over all the world, and that of others compared with it ascertained. To do so, however, with perfect effect requires the utmost care in the transport of the intermediate barometer, and is by no means an operation either of trifling import or of hurried or negligent performance: some of the greatest questions in meteorology depend on its due execution.

The next correction, and in some respects the most important of all, is that due to the temperature of the mercury in the barometer tube at the time of observation. To obtain this every barometer requires to have attached to it a thermometer, which in the instruments furnished to the observatories dips into the mercury in the cistern, and this must be read and registered at each observation of the barometer. In the appendix will be found a table calculated by Professor Schumacher, which gives for every degree of the thermometer and every half inch of the barometer, the proper quantity to be added or subtracted for the reduction of the observed height to the standard temperature of 32° Fahr.

It must, however, be observed, that this table is only calculated for barometers whose scales are engraven upon a rod or plate of brass reaching from the level of the mercury to the vernier. In many barometers the scale is engraved upon a short plate of brass fixed upon the wooden frame of the instrument, and the compound expansion of the two substances can only be guessed at, but must be obviously less than if the whole length had been of brass. As a near approximation for such imperfect instruments, another table has been placed in the appendix, in which the lesser expansion of glass has been substituted for that of brass. No scientific observer, however, would willingly use such an instrument.

Although all these corrections are necessary for the strict *reduction* of registered observations, they ought not to be applied to individual observations previously to registry. In the blank forms of register furnished to the observatories, one sheet is devoted to uncorrected observations, and a second to the corrected; and it is much to be wished that the proper reductions should be made as soon after the observations as possible.

2. THERMOMETERS.

Times of observation.—The external standard thermometer should be observed and registered at the same times as the barometer, and all the register thermometers may be read off at the time of the 9 A.M. observation, and their indices re-adjusted. But as double maxima frequently, and double minima occasionally, occur, in consequence of sudden changes of temperature, both the thermometers should be occasionally inspected with a view to ascertain whether the motion of either the mercury or the spirit has been reversed in an unusual manner; and such double maxima or minima should be recorded apart as *supernumerary*, with the dates and leading features of the case.

Each observatory has been furnished with a standard thermometer, of which duplicates have been deposited at the Royal Society, and which have been carefully compared with an authentic standard.

The spirit thermometers have been constructed with every possible attention to accuracy. A fixed point of temperature has been directly determined for each, at or about 0°, by means of a freezing mixture and comparison with a standard mercurial thermometer; and to render their indications accurate at still lower temperatures, the tubes are frustra of inverted cones, the rate of redaction of calibre being such as to compensate very nearly for the diminishing rate of the contraction of alcohol as we descend in the scale of temperature. For example, a column of mercury 5·10 inches long at the top of the instrument, changes to 5·40—5·43—5·46: the rapid change of the calibre at the top of the tube corresponding to the increased expansion of the spirits at the top of the scale. The specific gravity of the spirit employed is 822.

In general, however, accuracy would be most satisfactorily insured by selecting tubes of equal bores, and dividing the scales into equal degrees, which could be easily corrected, for the diminishing rate of the contraction of alcohol, by reference to proper tables.

It is recommended that all thermometers be carefully and frequently compared with the standard, and their differences, at one or more temperatures (the wider asunder the better), marked upon their scales and applied as index errors. This is particularly necessary with the register thermometers, whose construction renders them most liable to such errors.

In placing the standard thermometer, an exposure should be chosen perfectly shaded from the sun, one where no reflected sunbeams from water, buildings, rocks, or dry soil can reach it, and one which is easily accessible for observation. It should be *fixed*, not merely *hung*, upon a bracket projecting six inches from the wall, or other support to which it may be attached, and it must be *completely* sheltered from rain by a screen, so that the bulb shall never be wetted. In reading it, the observer should avoid touching, breathing on, or in any way warming it by near approach of his person; and in night observations particular care should be taken not to heat it by approximation of the light. The quicker the reading is done the better.

Notice should, of course, be taken of all sudden and remarkable changes of temperature, although such occasional observations must not be recorded in the regular series.

The self-registering thermometers should be placed with the same precautions as the standard, and so fastened as to allow of one end being detached, and lifted up to allow of the indices within the tubes sliding down to the ends of the fluid columns, which they will readily do with the assistance of occasional tapping.

The self-registering thermometers are apt to get out of order by the indices becoming entangled, or from the breaking of the column of fluid. When this happens with the spirit thermometer, it may be rectified with ease by jerking the index down to the junction of the bulb and tube. The whole of the tube will at the same time become wetted with the spirit; and by setting it on end with the bulb downwards, the spirit will run together into one continuous column.

When the steel index of the mercurial thermometer becomes immersed in the mercury, it must be jerked in the opposite direction, till it, with the mercury which may be above it, is projected into the little bulb at the top of the tube. If this do not succeed, heat must be applied to the mercury-bulb, and when the index is fairly lodged in the air-bulb, by carefully warming the mercury-bulb with a spirit lamp having a very small flame, the mercury must be made to expand till it rises to the very top of the tube, and projects convexly into the air-bulb. The tube must then be placed upright, and, by tapping, the detached mercury will slip down beneath the steel index, and will fairly unite with the convex projection aforesaid. Now let the bulb cool, and the mercury will sink in one united column, and leave the index free.

Besides the regular series of observations of the temperature of the air, there are other occasional observations to be made of temperature under different circumstances, which might possess great interest.

The surface temperature of the water of the sea or of rivers may be conveniently obtained by taking up a bucket-full of water and stirring round the thermometer in it.

The temperature of the water of deep wells may be ascertained in the same way, and should be taken monthly, if near the residence of the observer. The temperature of rain should also be attended to at times; it may be determined by receiving the rain in a *linen* funnel, totally enclosed in a tin case to prevent cooling by evaporation from the linen.

The temperature of the soil at different depths is a point of considerable importance. For this purpose excavations should be made in a dry sheltered situation, 3, 6, and 9 feet deep, and lined with brick or earthenware tubes. In the bottom of these excavations earthenware quart bottles may be carefully placed, filled with water, spirit, or brine, and corked. They must be carefully covered with tow or cotton, and drawn up on the 21st of every month (being the day of horary observation), and their temperatures taken by an accurate thermometer, and registered apart.

As a general caution it may be mentioned, that the *standard* thermometer should never be exposed to risk by application to such purposes, but thermometers which have been compared and corrected by comparison with it.

3. Actinometers.

Amongst the observations of highest importance must be ranked those of the force of solar and terrestrial radiation. The most perfect means of observing the former is afforded by the actinometer.

This instrument consists of a large hollow cylinder of glass, soldered at one end to a thermometer-tube, terminated at the upper end by a ball drawn out to a point, and broken off, so as to leave the end open. The other end of the cylinder is closed by a silver or silver-plated cap, cemented on it, and furnished with a screw, also of silver, passing through a collar of waxed leather, which is pressed into forcible contact with its thread, by a tightening-screw of large diameter enclosing it, and working into the silver cap, and driven home by the aid of a strong steel key or wrench, which accompanies the instrument.

The cylinder is filled with a deep blue liquid (ammonio-sulphate of copper), which ought to have been prepared some months beforehand, as it deposits a sediment when fresh, however clear or carefully filtered. This sediment, if deposited in the interior of the instrument, may be washed out with weak muriatic acid, which should itself be removed by water before refilling the instrument, and the ball at the top being purposely left full of air, and the point closed with melted wax, it becomes, in any given position of the screw, a thermometer of great delicacy, capable of being read off on a divided scale attached. The cylinder is enclosed in a chamber blackened on three sides, and on the fourth, or face, defended from currents of air by a thick glass, removeable at pleasure.

The action of the screw is to diminish or increase at pleasure the capacity of the hollow of the cylinder, and thus to drive, if necessary, a portion of the liquid up into the ball, which acts as a reservoir, or, if necessary, to draw back from the reservoir such a quantity as shall just fill it, leaving no bubble of air in the cylinder.

To use the instrument, examine first whether there be any air in the cylinder, which is easily seen by holding it level, and tilting it, when the air, if any, will be seen to run along it. If there be any, hold it upright in the left hand, and the air will ascend to the root of the thermometer-tube. Then, by alternate screwing and unscrewing the screw with the right hand, as the case may require, it will always be practicable to drive the air out of the cylinder into the ball, and suck down liquid, if any, from the ball, to supply its place, till the air is entirely evacuated from the cylinder, and the latter, as well as the whole stem of the thermometer-tube, is full of the liquid in an unbroken column. Then, holding it horizontally, face upwards, slowly and cautiously unscrew the screw, till the liquid retreats to the zero of the scale.

The upper bulb is drawn out into a fine tube, which is stopped with wax. When it is needed to empty, cleanse, and refill the instrument, liquid must first be forced up into the ball, so as to compress the air in it. On warming the end, the wax will be forced out, and the screw being then totally unscrewed, and the liquid poured out, the interior of the instrument may be washed with water slightly acidulated, and the tube, ball, &c. cleansed, in the same way, after which the wax must be replaced, and the instrument refilled.

To make an observation with the actinometer, the observer must station himself in the sunshine, or in some sharply terminated shadow, so that without inconvenience, or materially altering his situation, or the exposure of the instrument in other respects, he can hold it at pleasure, either in full sun or total shadow. If placed in the sun, he must provide himself with a screen of pasteboard or tin plate, large enough to shade the whole of the lower part or chamber of the instrument, which should be placed not less than two feet from the instrument, and should be removeable in an instant of time. The best station is a room with closed doors, before an open window, or under an opening in the roof into which the sun shines freely. Draughts of air should be prevented as much as possible. If the observations be made out of doors, shelter from gusts of wind and freedom from all penumbral shadows, as of ropes, rigging, branches, &c. should be sought. Generally, the more the observer is at his ease, with his watch and writing-table beside him, the better. He should have a watch or chronometer beating at least twice in a second, and provided with a second hand; also a pencil and paper ruled, according to the form subjoined, for registering the observations. Let him then grasp the instrument in his left hand, or if he have a proper stand (which is preferable on shore or in a building*), otherwise firmly support it, so as to expose its face perpendicularly to the direct rays of the sun, as exactly as may be.

The liquid, as soon as exposed, will mount rapidly in the stem. It should be allowed to do so for three or four minutes before the observation begins, taking care, however, not to let it mount into the bulb, by a proper use of the screw. At the same time the tube should be carefully cleared (by the same action) of all small broken portions of liquid remaining in it, which should all be drawn down into the bulb. When all is ready for observation, draw the liquid down to zero of its scale, gently and steadily; place it on its stand, with its screen before it, and proceed as follows.

Having previously ascertained how many times (suppose 20) the watch beats in five seconds, let the screen be withdrawn at ten seconds before a complete minute shown by the watch, suppose at 2^h 14^m 50^s. From 50^s to 55^s, say 0, 0, 0, ... at each beat of the watch, looking meanwhile that all is right. At 55^s complete, count 0, 1, 2, ... up to 20 beats, or to the whole minute, 2^h 15^m 0^s, keeping the eye not on the watch, but on the end of the rising column of liquid. At the 20th beat read off, and register the reading ($12°·0$), as in column 3, A, of the annexed form. Then wait, watching the column of air above the liquid, to see that no blebs of liquid are in it, or at the opening of the upper bulb (which will cause the movement of the ascending column to be performed by starts), till the minute is nearly elapsed. At the 50th second begin to watch the liquid rising; at 55^s begin to count 0, 1, 2, up to 20 beats, as before, attentively

---

* This may consist of two deal boards, 18 inches long, connected by a hinge, and kept at any required angle by an iron, pointed at each end. The upper should have a little rabbet or moulding fitting loosely round the actinometer, to prevent its slipping off.

1.		2.	3.		4.	5.	6.
Date and times of observation. Feldhausen, 1837, Oct. 30.		Exposure, sun ⊙ or shade ×.	Readings of the instrument.		Change per minute. B − A.	Radiation in parts of scale.	Remarks.
Initial.	Terminal.		A. Initial.	B. Terminal.			
h m s 2 15 0	m s 16 0	⊙	+ 12·0	+ 43·3	+ 31·3	....	⎰ The times are reduced to *appa-*
16 30	17 30	×	45·2	42·8	− 2·4	34·75	⎱ *rent* time, or to the sun's hour angle from the meridian.
18 0	19 0	⊙	14·8	48·2	+ 33·4	35·40	Zero withdrawn.
19 30	20 30	×	28·0	26·8	− 1·4	34·85	
21 0	22 0	⊙	9·4	43·9	+ 33·5	34·75	
22 30	23 30	×	46·6	45·5	− 1·1	34·95	⎰ General mean per formula = 34·73
24 0	25 0	⊙	9·0	43·2	+ 34·2	....	⎱ for 2ʰ 20ᵐ 0ˢ of apparent time.

watching the rise of the liquid; and at the 20th beat, or complete minute ($2^h 16^m 0^s$) read off, and instantly shade the instrument, or withdraw it *just out* of the sun and penumbra. Then register the reading off ($43°3$) in column 3, B, and prepare for the shade observation. All this may be done without hurry in 20 seconds, with time also to withdraw the screw if the end of the column be inconveniently high in the scale, which is often required. At the 20th second prepare to observe; at the 25th begin to count beats, 0, 1, 2, ... 20; and at the 20th beat, i. e. at $2^h 16^m 30^s$, read off, and enter the reading in column 3, A, as the initial shade reading ($45°·2$). Then wait as before till nearly a minute has elapsed, and at $2^h 17^m 20^s$ again prepare. At $17^m 25^s$ begin to count beats; at $17^m 30^s$ read off, and enter this *terminal* shade reading ($42°·8$) in column 3, B, and if needed, withdraw the zero.

Again wait 20^s, in which interval there is time for the entry, &c. At $17^m 50^s$ remove the screen, or expose the instrument in the sun; at 55^s begin to count beats; and at the complete minute, $18^m 0^s$, read off ($14°·8$), and so on for several alternations, *taking care to begin and end each series with a sun observation*. If the instrument be held in the hand, care should be taken not to change the inclination of its axis to the horizon between the readings, or the compressibility of the liquid by its own weight will produce a very appreciable amount of error.

In the annexed form column 1. contains the times, initial and terminal of each sun and shade observation. Column 2. expresses by an appropriate mark, ⊙ and ×, the exposure, whether in sun or shade. Column 3. contains the readings, initial and terminal (A and B). Column 4. gives the values of B − A, with its algebraical sign expressing the rise and fall per minute. And here it may be observed, that if by forgetfulness the exact minute be passed, the reading off may be made at the next 10^s, and in that case the entry in column 4 must be not the *whole* amount of B − A, but only $\frac{6}{7}$ths of that amount, so as to reduce it to an interval of 60^s precise. Column 5. contains the radiations as derived from successive triplets, $\odot \times \odot$, $\times \odot \times$, $\odot \times \odot$, &c. by the formula presently to be stated; and in column 6. are entered remarks, such as the state of the sky, wind, &c.; as also (when taken) the sun's altitude, barometer, thermometer, and other readings, &c.

The formula of reduction is as follows. Let $\odot$, $\times$, $\odot'$, $\times'$, $\odot''$, $\times''$, &c. represent the numbers in column 4, with their signs in order, as they stand, or the values of $B - A$. Then will the numbers in column 5 be respectively,

$$+ \frac{\odot + \odot'}{2} - \times$$

$$- \frac{\times + \times'}{2} + \odot'$$

$$+ \frac{\odot' + \odot''}{2} - \times'$$

$$- \frac{\times' + \times''}{2} + \odot'',$$

and so on, the algebraic signs being carefully attended to. Thus

$$34{\cdot}75 = + \frac{31{\cdot}3 + 33{\cdot}4}{2} + 2{\cdot}4$$

$$35{\cdot}40 = + \frac{2{\cdot}4 + 1{\cdot}4}{2} + 33{\cdot}4, \text{ &c.}$$

The mean of a series not exceeding three or four triplets may be had by the formula

$$\frac{\odot + \odot' + \odot'' + \text{&c.}}{n} - \frac{\times + \times' + \text{&c.}}{n - 1},$$

where n is the number of sun observations, the time corresponding being the middle of the middle shade observation.

A complete actinometer observation cannot consist of less than three sun and two shade observations intermediate; but the more there are taken the better, and in a very clear sunny day it is highly desirable to continue the alternate observations for a long time, even from sunrise to sunset, so as to deduce by a graphical projection the law of diurnal increase and diminution of the solar radiation, which will thus readily become apparent, provided the perfect clearness of the sky continue,—an indispensable condition in these observations, the slightest cloud or haze over the sun being at once marked by a diminution of resulting radiation.

To detect such haze or cirrus, a brown glass applied before the eye is useful, and by the help of such a glass it may here be noticed that solar halos are very frequently to be seen when the glare of light is such as to allow nothing of the sort to be perceived by the unguarded eye.

It is, as observed, essential that the instrument be exposed a few minutes to the sun, to raise its temperature in some slight degree. If this be not done, owing to some cause not very obvious, the first triplet of observations (sun, shade, sun) will give a radiation perceptibly in defect of the truth, as will become distinctly apparent on continuing the series. But it may be as well for a beginner to commence at once reading as soon as the instrument is exposed, and reject the first two triplets, by which he will see whether he has all his apparatus conveniently arranged, and get settled at his post.

When a series is long continued in a good sun, the instrument grows very hot, and the rise of the liquid in the sun observation decreases, while the fall in the shade increases; nay, towards sunset it will fall even in the sun. This phenomenon (which is at first startling, and seeming to impeach the fidelity of the instrument) is, in fact, perfectly in order, and produces absolutely no irregularity in the resulting march of the radiation. Only it is necessary in casting up the result (in col. 5.) to attend carefully to the algebraic signs of the differences in column 4, as in the following example (which, as well as that above given, is one of actual occurrence).

1.		2.	3.		4.	5.	6.
Date and times of observation. Wynberg, Nov. 24, 1837.		Exposure, sun or shade.	Readings of the Instrument.		Change per minute B − A.	Radiation in parts of scale.	Remarks.
Initial.	Terminal.		A. Initial.	B. Terminal.			
h m s	m s						
6 5 15	....	...	....	....	....	....	Alt. of ☉ = 7° 19′.
9 0	10 0	☉	+ 9·0	+ 9·7	+ 0·7		
10 30	11 30	x	23·0	10·8	− 12·2	11·25	
12 0	13 0	☉	34·0	31·4	− 2·6	9·25	
13 30	14 30	x	28·5	17·0	− 11·5	8·20	Cirrous haze coming on.
15 0	16 0	☉	12·0	8·0	− 4·0		
6 19 15	....	...	....	....	....	....	Alt. of ☽ = 4° 37′.

Every series of actinometer observations should be accompanied with notices in the column of remarks of the state of the wind and sky generally, the approach of any cloud (as seen in the coloured glass) near to the sun; the barometer and thermometers, *dry* and *wet*, should especially be read off more than once during the series, if a long one, and, if kept up during several hours, hourly. The times should be correct to the nearest minute, at least as serving to calculate the sun's altitude; but if this be taken (to the nearest minute or two) with a pocket sextant, or even by a style and shadow, frequently (at intervals of an hour or less) when the sun is rising or setting, it will add much to the immediate interest of the observations. When the sun is near the horizon, its reflection from the sea, or any neighbouring water, must be prevented from striking on the instrument; and similarly of snow in cold regions, or on great elevations in alpine countries.

Every actinometer should be provided with a spare glass, and all the glasses should be marked with a diamond; and it should always be noted at the head of the column of remarks; which glass is used, as the co-efficient of reduction from the parts of the scale (which are arbitrary) to parts of the *unit of radiation* varies with the glass used.

In the case of the actinometers sent out with the Expedition and to the fixed observatories, it was not practicable to ascertain these co-efficients for each instrument and each glass owing to the total absence of any favourable opportunity of sunshine. The values of the parts of the respective scales of the instruments, as determined approximatively by careful measurement of the dimensions, were as follows :—

Marks of the Actinometers.		Multiplier for reducing parts observed to parts of a standard retained in possession, marked A 1.	Approximate value of one part of scale in Actines.
Maker's Mark.	Private Mark.		
1	K	1·4909	7·085
2	L	1·3726	6·523
3	M	1·4020	6·663
A 4	N	1·6550	7·864
A 5	O	1·4403	6·844
6	P	1·0608	5·041

The dimensions of the instruments which are used in these reductions are,

1st. The external diameter of the cylinder containing the coloured liquid, i. e. its mean diameter, if on measurement with fine callipers its two ends be found to differ.

2nd. The length of that portion of it which receives the sunbeam.

The product of these two data gives the area of the section of the sunbeam effective in raising the temperature, and which, though not all *equally* effective, by reason of the cylindrical form of the glass, is yet effective in *the same ratio* in all of them by reason of their general similarity of figure. At the magnetical observatories the dew point will be observed at the nearest *magnetical* hours to the *meteorological* hours above fixed on (3 and 9 A.M. and P.M.).

3rd. The content (in water grains) of 100 parts in length of the capillary tube used for the scale. This may best be determined by gauging it with mercury before it is soldered to the cylinder, and ought always to be so determined by the maker; but when fitted, this is impracticable, and the measurement of the element in question must be performed as follows :—

The instrument being placed horizontally, and allowed to attain the precise temperature of the apartment, let the liquid be brought to zero by the motion of the screw; after which let the screw be turned precisely one revolution, or half revolution (as the scale may require) *in*, and note the rise of the liquid in parts of the scale. This must be done several times, alternately screwing *in* and *out*. The screw must then be taken out; its threads counted, and the weight of water displaced from a narrow vessel exactly full, by the immersion of the whole length occupied by the thread exactly ascertained by a nice balance; after which a very simple calculation will give the value of the parts of the scale in water grains required; this process was followed in the case of the instruments above mentioned, and if carefully conducted is susceptible of great precision.

The glasses as well as the cylinders and capillary stems of the instruments, if accidentally broken, should have their fragments carefully preserved and labelled.

The unit of solar radiation to be adopted in the ultimate reduction of the actinometric observations is the *actine*, by which is understood that intensity of solar radiation, which at a vertical incidence, and supposing it wholly absorbed, would suffice to melt one millionth part of a metre in thickness, from the surface of a sheet of ice horizontally exposed to its action per minute of mean solar time; but it will be well to reserve the reduction of the radiations as expressed in parts of the scale to their values in terms of their unit until the final discussion of the observations.

Meanwhile, no opportunities should be lost of *comparing* together the indications of different actinometers under similar and favourable circumstances, so as to establish a correspondence of scales, which in case of accident happening to one of the instruments, will preserve its registered observations from loss.

The comparison of two actinometers may be executed by one observer using alternately each of the two instruments, thus,

Instrument A.	Instrument B.	A.	Etc.
⊙.. ..	⊙....	⊙.	
✕.. .	✕.. : .	✕....... .	
⊙.... .	⊙.... .	⊙.. ...	

beginning and ending with the same; though it would be more conveniently done by two observers observing simultaneously at the same place, and each registering his own instrument. An hour or two thus devoted to comparisons in a calm clear day, and under easy circumstances, will in all cases be extremely well bestowed.

Neither should each observer neglect to determine for himself the heat stopped by each of his glasses. This may be done also by alternating triplets of observation made with the glass on and off, thus,

Glass off.	Glass on.	Glass off.	Etc.
⊙........	⊙.... ..	⊙.......	
✕........	✕.. ...	✕........	
⊙....	⊙..	⊙........	

beginning and ending with the glass off, and (as in all cases) beginning and ending each *triplet* with a sun observation. For the purpose now in question a very *calm* day must be chosen, and a great many triplets must be taken in succession. It will be found that a single thickness of the ordinary bluish or greenish plate glass stops about 0·20 (= $\frac{1}{5}$) of the incident calorific rays; a second glass about 0·16 (or a materially less proportion) of those which have escaped the action of the first. No two glasses, however, are precisely alike in this respect.

Very interesting observations may be made by two observers furnished with well-compared actinometers, the one stationed at the summit, the other at the foot of some great elevation, especially if the stations can be so selected that the observers shall be nearly in the line of the incident sunbeam at the time of observation, so as both to lie in the atmospheric column traversed by the rays. Many convenient stations of this kind might be found in mountainous countries; and by repeating the observation two or three times under favorable circumstances, interchanging observers and instruments, &c., and accompanying the observations with all circumstantial and local elements of precision, there is no doubt that the co-efficient of extinction of solar heat in traversing at least the lower strata of our atmosphere might be obtained with much exactness, and thus a highly valuable datum secured to science. The observers would, of course, agree to make their observations strictly simultaneous, and should, therefore, compare watches before parting.

The actinometer is also well calculated for measuring the defalcation of heat during any considerable eclipse of the sun, and the Council would point out this as an object worthy of attention, both at the fixed stations and on board the vessels; as many eclipses invisible or insignificant in one locality, are great, or even total in others. The observations should commence an hour at least before the eclipse begins, and be continued an hour beyond its termination, and the series should be uninterrupted, leaving to others to watch the phases of the eclipse. The atmospheric circumstances should be most carefully noted during the whole series.

Though out of the question in the circumstances immediately under contemplation, it may not be amiss to remind aeronauts, that observations of the actinometer may, no doubt, be made with considerable ease and precision in the car of a balloon, and if accompanied with good barometric and hygrometric simultaneous observations aloft and below would in every point of view be most precious, thus adding one to the many useful subjects of inquiry in those hitherto almost useless adventures.

4. Radiating Thermometers.

As, however, the actinometer can only be observed at intervals in perfectly clear weather, additional information with regard to solar radiation, of much interest, though not of so precise a nature, may be obtained, by the daily register of the maximum temperature of a register thermometer, with a blackened bulb exposed to the full action of the sun's rays. It may be placed about an inch above the bare soil, and screened from currents of air. The maximum temperature indicated by such a thermometer, even in cloudy weather, will generally be considerably above that of the air, and the maxima and mean daily maxima of its indications will, after a long series of observations, afford data of the utmost value to the history of climates. The bulb of the thermometer should be about half an inch in diameter, and it may be uniformly blackened with lamp-black and varnish. The graduation should be made upon the glass stem, to prevent any inconvenience from the expansion and warping of the scale.

The measure of terrestrial radiation is of no less importance to the science of meteorology than that of solar radiation, but no perfect instrument has yet been contrived for its determination. Very valuable information, however, may be derived from the daily register of the minimum temperature of a register spirit-thermometer, the bulb of which is placed in the focus of a parabolic metallic mirror, turned towards the clear aspect of the sky, and screened from currents. The mirrors furnished to the observatories are of silver-plated copper, but planished tin-plate or zinc might be substituted without detriment. They are 6 inches diameter and 2 inches deep, and the thermometers which are graduated upon the stems pass through sockets in their sides, in which they may be accurately adjusted by corks. Their bulbs do not exceed half an inch in diameter.

Even in the daytime a thermometer so placed, and turned towards the clear sky, but away from the rays of the sun, will fall several degrees below the temperature of the surrounding air.

5. HYGROMETERS.

Times of observation.—Observations of the *dew-point* hygrometer are as desirable at the regular hours as those of the other meteorological instruments; but, as more difficulty attends the observation, it is more liable to omission, and it is of great importance that when one experiment only can be made, the most advantageous hour should be selected for the purpose. Now it is probable that the minimum temperature of the air in the 24 hours may correspond with the minimum temperature of the dew-point; and for the attainment of a mean result, the time of the highest dew-point should be selected, which would not differ much from 3 P.M., at which hour the observation should on no account be omitted. The hygrometer should also be observed, if possible, at 9 A.M. and 9 P.M., but the minimum temperature might probably be substituted for the 3 A.M. observation without any material error.

At the magnetical observatories the dew-point will be observed at the nearest *magnetical* hours to the *meteorological* hours above fixed on (3 and 9 A.M. and P.M.).

Occasional observations of the dew-point under peculiar circumstances, as for instance in the inhabited apartments of houses or between the decks of the ships when laid up in their winter quarters in the polar regions, could not but afford information of high practical importance.

All the ether of the dew-point hygrometer should be driven by the warmth of the hand from the covered ball into the uncovered, previously to an observation, and the ether should be dropped from a dropping-bottle very slowly upon the former. The temperature of the interior thermometer should be carefully noted upon the first appearance of the ring of dew upon the black bulb, and also its temperature upon its disappearance: the mean of the two observations, should they differ, may be entered as the dew-point, together with the temperature of the air by the exterior thermometer.

The *wet-bulb* hygrometer can be observed without difficulty, by mere inspection, and the observation should never be neglected at the regular hours. It is probable that the temperature of evaporation thus ascertained may afford the means of accurately determining the dew-point, and of solving all the points of hygrometry; but until all the necessary corrections shall have been agreed upon, one of the most essential requisites must be its frequent and accurate comparison with the dew-point, directly ascertained.

The instruments supplied to the observatories are fitted with waterholders for keeping the bulb of the thermometer moist; but it should be observed, that the floss-silk, after being some time in use, has its faculty of conducting moisture greatly diminished, if not destroyed, and therefore requires to be renewed from time to time. When proper time can be afforded to allow the thermometer to take up its stationary temperature, it is, perhaps, best to moisten the ball for each observation. By urging upon the wet bulb a jet of air from a small double-bellows, the maximum depression may be obtained in a few seconds. In fact, the formula $f'' = f' - \dfrac{d}{88} \times \dfrac{30}{p-f}$ investigated by Dr. Apjohn, was tested under these circumstances, and he is of opinion that there will always be a small difference between the depression occurring in air at rest, and sweeping by the thermometer in a rapid current.

In this formula, f'' is the tension of steam at the dew-point; f' its tension at the temperature of the hygrometer; d the depression, or difference between the hygrometer and the air; 88 a coefficient depending upon the specific heat of air and the caloric of electricity of its included vapour; p the existing and 30 the mean pressure of the air.

The hygrometers should be placed in the observatory, near to the standard thermometer, with which they should be frequently compared.

6. Vanes, Anemometers, and Rain Gauges.

The magnetic observatories and the Antarctic Expedition have been furnished with Osler's self-registering anemometer and raingauge.

In this instrument the direction of the wind is obtained by means of the vane attached to the rod, or rather tube, that carries it, and consequently causes the latter to move with itself. At the lower extremity of this tube is a small pinion working in a rack, which slides backwards and forwards, as the wind moves the vane; and to this rack a pencil is attached, which marks the direction of the wind on a paper ruled with the cardinal points, and so adjusted as to progress at the rate of 1 inch per hour, by means of a clock; the force is at the same time ascertained by a plate 1 foot square, placed at right angles to the vane, supported by two light bars running on friction-rollers, and communicating with three spiral springs in such a way that the plate cannot be affected by the wind's pressure without instantly acting on the springs, and communicating the quantum of its action by a wire passing down the centre of the tube, to another pencil below, which thus registers its degree of force. The rain is registered at the same time by its weight acting on a balance, which moves in proportion to the quantity falling, and has also a pencil attached to it, recording the results. The receiver is so arranged as to discharge every half inch that falls, when the pencil again starts at zero.

It is probable that the results obtained with this instrument would require correction for the varying effects of the eddy, which must be formed behind the board before they can be considered as exact measures of the pressure; and the effects of variations of temperature upon the force of the springs should be experimentally ascertained, particularly in very cold climates. This latter point may be determined by measuring the compression directly by the application of known weights.

Another self-registering anemometer has recently been constructed by Professor Whewell, which exhibits upon a diagram not only the direction and force, but the direction and integral effect of the wind, but which is more complex in its construction, and practically more liable to derangement.

In it a small set of windmill vanes, something like the ventilators of windows, are presented to the wind by a common vane, in whatever direction it may blow. The current, as it passes, sets these vanes in rapid motion, and a train of wheels and pinions reduces the motion, which is thence communicated to a pencil traversing vertically, and pressing against an upright cylinder, which forms the support of the instrument: 1000 revolutions of the fly only cause the pencil to descend $\frac{1}{20}$th of an inch. The surface of the cylinder is covered with white paper, and the pencil, as the vane wavers, keeps tracing a thick irregular line, like the shadings on the coast of a map. The middle of the line may be easily traced, and it gives the mean direction of the wind, while the length of the line is proportional to the velocity of the wind and the length of time during which it blows in each direction.

Those who do not possess a register-anemometer may make use of the common vane and Lind's wind-gauge. The position of the former should be clear of all deflections and eddies from objects of the same or a higher level, and of course its position with regard to the true north should be clearly determined. In registering the direction of the wind it may be sufficient to use only 16 points of the compass.

Lind's wind-gauge for measuring the force or momentum of the wind is adjusted for use by filling it with water till the liquid in both legs of the siphon corresponds with the 0° of the scale. It is to be held perpendicularly, with the mouth of the kneed tube turned towards the wind, and the amount of the depression in one leg, and that of its elevation in the other, are to be carefully noted. The sum of the two is the height of a column of water which the wind is capable of sustaining at the time, and every body that is opposed to that wind will be pressed upon by a force equivalent to the weight of a column of water, having its base equal to the surface that is opposed, and its height equal to the altitude of the column of water sustained by the wind in the wind-gauge.

The height of this column being given, the force of the wind on a foot square is easily found by a table which will be given in the appendix.

The observation of the gauge should always be made at the same point of a free space, and in gusty weather the maximum of the oscillation recorded. The most proper periods will be those of the other regular observations; but in great storms, or under other particular circumstances, occasional observations should be made, and registered apart.

Even in observatories which are provided with Osler's apparatus it is desirable that an accurate comparison should be made of the two anemometers.

The points most important to remark respecting the wind are,

1st. Its average intensity and general direction during the several portions of the day devoted to observation.

2ndly. The hours of the day or night when it commences to blow from a calm, or subsides into one from a breeze.

3rdly. The hours at which any remarkable changes of its direction take place.

4thly. The course which it takes in veering, and the quarter in which it ultimately settles.

5thly. The usual course of *periodical winds,* or such as remarkably prevail during certain seasons, with the law of their diurnal progress, both as to direction and intensity; at what hours, and by what degrees they commence, attain their maximum, and subside; and through what points of the compass they run in so doing.

6thly. The existence of crossing currents at different heights in the atmosphere, as indicated by the courses of the clouds in different strata.

7thly. The times of setting-in of remarkably hot or cold winds, the quarters from which they come, and their courses, as connected with the progressive changes in their temperature.

8thly. The connexion of rainy, cloudy or fair weather, with the quarter from which the wind blows, or has blown for some time previously.

The Rain-gauge may be of very simple construction. A cubical box of strong tin or zinc, exactly 10 inches by the side, open above, receives at an inch below its edge a funnel, sloping to a small hole in the centre. On one of the lateral edges of the box, close to the top of the cavity, is soldered a short pipe, in which a cork is fitted. The whole should be well painted. The water which enters this gauge is poured through the short tube into a cylindrical glass ves sel, graduated to cubic inches and fifths of cubic inches. Hence one inch depth of rain in the gauge will be measured by 100 inches of the graduated vessel, and $\frac{1}{100}$th inch of rain may be very easily read off.

It is very much to be desired that, being of such easy construction, more than one of these gauges should be erected, or at least one placed with its edge nearly level with the ground, and another upon the top of the highest building, rock, or tree in the immediate vicinity of the place of observation, the height of which must be carefully determined; it having been satisfactorily ascertained that the height of the gauge above the ground is a very material element in the quantity of rain which enters it. The quantity of water should be daily measured and registered at 9 A.M.

7. Clouds and Meteors.

Many very highly-interesting observations may be made, without the aid of instruments, upon the clouds. In describing them Mr. Howard's nomenclature may be adopted with great advantage. By means of the clouds different simultaneous currents of wind may often be detected, the different directions of which should be carefully ascertained by referring their motions to some fixed object. Their gradual evaporation or precipitation should also be carefully noted, and particularly their regular disappearance at night, or their more irregular and sudden formation.

Rainbows, parhelia, haloes, &c., will of course be noted amongst the occasional remarks of the register; and an attempt should be made to express approximatively by numbers, the proportion which the overcast portion of the sky may bear to the clear space. For this the hemisphere may be supposed to be divided into eight sections, and the cloudy portion may be expressed by the fraction $\frac{1}{8}$th or $\frac{5}{8}$ths, &c.

8. Electrometers.

The Council are fully impressed with the high importance of regular observations on the electrical state of the atmosphere; but they are not prepared to suggest any means of effecting this desirable object, which will at all correspond with the present advanced state of electrical physics. At no distant period they hope to see supplied a defect which is certainly a reproach to science. In the meantime much valuable information might be acquired by observations of an electroscope, on one of the ordinary constructions connected with a lofty insulated wire.

In erecting such a wire, proper precautions should be taken against accidents by preparing a sufficient conductor in its immediate vicinity, by which a communication could be at once opened with the ground in case of any sudden and dangerous accumulation of the electric fluid.

As a temporary contrivance, a common jointed fishing-rod, having a glass stick well varnished with shell lac, substituted for its smallest joint, may be projected into the atmosphere. To the end of the glass must be fixed a metallic wire terminating in a point, and connected with an electroscope by means of a fine copper wire. If the wire be made to terminate in a spiral wrapped round a piece of cotton dipped in spirits of wine and inflamed, its power of collecting electricity will be sometimes doubled, but great precautions are necessary when this mode is employed. When the electroscope has been charged, the nature of the electricity may be tested in the usual way by excited glass or sealing wax.

The principal electroscopes which are capable of being employed to ascertain the electrical state of the atmosphere, or rather to compare its state at any given elevation with the state of the medium in contact with the instrument, are the following.

1. De Saussure's electrometer, which consists of two fine wires, each terminated by a small pith ball, and adapted to a small metal rod fixed in the upper part of a square glass cover, upon one of the faces of which a divided scale is marked, in order to measure the angles of deviation of the two balls.

2. Volta's electrometer, formed of two straws about 2 inches long and $\frac{1}{4}$th of a line broad, suspended from two small very moveable rings adapted to a metal rod: to measure the deviation of the straws a telescope with a nonius is employed.

3. Singer's electrometer, consisting of two slips of gold leaf suspended from the rod.

4. Bohnenberger's electroscope, formed of a single strip of gold leaf suspended from the conducting rod between two dry piles, the negative pole of one and the positive pole of the other being uppermost: this arrangement has the advantage of indicating the kind of electricity communicated to the conductor.

The observations made with these and similar instruments have demonstrated that in serene weather the electricity of the atmosphere is always positive with regard to that of the earth, and that it becomes more and more positive in proportion to its elevation above the earth's surface; so that if an observer be on a mountain or in a balloon, if his conductor be directed downwards to reach an inferior stratum of air, his electroscope will indicate negative electricity; and if it be sent upwards into a superior stratum, positive electricity will be manifested. Various means have been resorted to in these experiments, such as connecting one of the extremities of the conducting wire to a kite, a small balloon, or the head of an arrow, the other extremity remaining attached to the electroscope.

It has been ascertained by the observations of De Saussure, Schubler, Arago and others, that the positive electricity of the atmosphere is subject to diurnal variations of intensity, there being two maxima and two minima during the twenty-four hours. The first minimum takes place a little before the rising of the sun; as it rises, the intensity, at first gradually and then rapidly, increases, and arrives at its first maximum a few hours after. This excess diminishes at first rapidly and afterwards slowly, and arrives at its minimum some hours before sunset; it re-ascends when the sun approaches the horizon, and attains its second maximum a few hours after, then diminishes till sunrise, and proceeds in the order already indicated. The intensity of the free electricity of the atmosphere has also been found to undergo annual changes, increasing from the month of July to the month of November inclusive, so that the greatest intensity occurs in winter, and the least in summer.

In cloudy weather the free electricity of the atmosphere is still positive. During storms, or when it rains or snows, the electricity is sometimes positive and sometimes negative, and its intensity is always much more considerable than in serene weather. The electroscope will, during the continuance of a storm, frequently indicate several changes, from positive to negative.

The above is a short summary of almost all that is known respecting the laws of atmospheric electricity. It will be highly important to obtain a series of observations equal in accuracy to those made by Schubler at Frankfort in 1811 and 1812, simultaneously with the observations of the hygrometer, barometer, thermometer, &c. Combined observations at a number of different stations cannot fail to give us important information respecting the distribution of the free electricity in the atmosphere, and the extent and nature of the disturbances to which it is subject; but to render the results valuable it will be necessary to have instruments comparable with each other, and this may be a difficult matter to effect*.

Very recently a new method of investigating the electric state of the atmosphere has been proposed, likely to lead hereafter to very certain and valuable results; but it has not been sufficiently put in practice to enable the Council to recommend, at the present moment, the best form of instrument for making simultaneous and comparable observations, or the proper precautions to guide the observer in manipulating it.

For the principle of this instrument we are indebted to Mr. Colladon of Geneva. He found, that if the two ends of the wire of a galvanic multiplier, consisting of very numerous coils well insulated from each other, were brought in contact, one with a body positively, and the other with a body negatively charged, a current of electricity passes through the wire, until equilibrium is restored; the energy and direction of this current is indicated by the deviation of the needle from the zero-point of the scale. This instrument is applied to the purpose of ascertaining and measuring the atmospheric electricity, by communicating one end of the wire with the earth, and allowing the other to extend into the region of the atmosphere, the electrical state of which is intended to be compared.

Thunder storms, of course, should be attended to; but it is of con-

---

* For a fuller account of what is known respecting atmospheric electricity, and the mode of conducting the observations, see Becquerel's *Traité de l'Electricité*, t. iv. pp. 78—125.

sequence also to notice distant lightning not accompanied with thunder audible at the place of observation, especially if it take place many days in succession, and to note the quarter of the horizon where it appears, and the extent which it embraces. In an actual thunder storm, especial notice should be taken of the quantity of rain which falls, and of the fits or intermittences of its fall, as corresponding, or not, to great bursts of lightning, as also of the direction of the wind, and the apparent progress of the storm with or against it *.

9. REGISTERS.

The Register proposed by the Council may be comprised in two skeleton forms, which have been supplied to the magnetical observatories and to the Expedition. This, it will be observed, applies to the meteorological forms about to be specified, independent of the more extensive and general forms for the registry of the magnetic observations, with their accompanying meteorological entries, with which the magnetical observatories will be supplied.

They are each calculated for one month's observation. *The first form* is for the insertion of observations as they are made in their uncorrected state. It consists of 12 principal divisions, and is ruled across for 31 days, and for the arithmetical convenience of casting up the sums and means of the quantities inserted. At the bottom of the sheet there is also a space provided for the hourly observations of the barometer and thermometers on *the twenty-first day of the month*, which will be more particularly described after the explanation of the principal divisions.

The outside compartments, both on the left and right of the sheet, are for the date of the month and the phases of the moon.

The second compartment is for the height of the barometer, and the temperature of the mercury for the four regular periods of observation.

The third compartment is appropriated to the dew-point hygrometer, and contains also four columns for the four daily observations, each of which is subdivided into three; for the temperature of the air, the dew-point, and the difference between the two.

The fourth compartment is for the wet-bulb hygrometer, and is similarly divided and subdivided for the temperature of the dry- and wet-bulb thermometer, and for their differences.

The fifth compartment is prepared for the maxima and minima of temperature, and is divided into three. In the first division are to be recorded the maxima and minima of thermometers carefully placed in the shade and screened from radiation. In the second, the maxima of a blackened thermometer exposed to the sun, and the minima of a thermometer placed in a metallic mirror, and radiating freely to the clear sky. The third is devoted to occasional observations of the actinometer under favourable circumstances.

The sixth compartment is for the temperature of the surface-water

* On these subjects the Council especially recommend the attentive perusal of Arago's *Notice sur le Tonnerre.*

of the sea, or of any river in the immediate neighbourhood of the observatory.

The seventh compartment is prepared for observations upon the direction and force of the wind at the four regular hours of registry In the left-hand column of each division is to be recorded the direction of the vane, and in the right-hand column the height of Lind's gauge, in tenths of an inch of water.

In the eighth compartment the amount of rain is to be registered once in the day; and in the ninth, the electrical state of the atmosphere, if possible, at the four periods, 3 A.M., 9 A.M., 3 P.M., and 9 P.M.

The tenth compartment is appropriated to remarks on the clouds, and weather generally; and in the eleventh is to be noted, at noon, the longitude and latitude at sea.

On a careful review of the month's observations, the maxima and minima results should have the algebraic signs + and — respectively affixed.

The second form is devoted to the corrected results of the observations, and to the optical comparison together of some of them, by their projection upon a scale of equal parts.

The upper half of the sheet is vertically divided into two equal parts, each prepared for half the month's observations, and accordingly ruled across into sixteen spaces for the daily observations, and two for the sums and means of the quantities. Each half is also divided into five compartments.

The first is for the date of the month and the phases of the moon.

The second for the corrected height of the barometer at 32° Fahr.

The third is appropriated to the elastic force of the aqueous vapour corresponding to the dew-point, and which may be taken from Table 5. in the Appendix B.

The fourth is for the maximum and minimum of temperature, and the mean of the two.

And the fifth for occasional remarks.

The lower half of the sheet is also vertically divided into two equal parts, each of which is similarly divided into 31 columns for the daily observations of a month; and these again subdivided into four, for the six-hourly observations of each day. The vertical lines thus formed are divided into 6 inches; and each inch into tenths of an inch, and half-tenths, by horizontal lines.

The left-hand compartment thus ruled, is intended for the projection of curves of temperature: for this purpose each tenth of an inch upon the scale must be reckoned a degree, which will be divided by the faint line into halves.

The value of the degree may be arbitrarily fixed, and inserted in the margin according to convenience. Towards the upper part of the scale the results of the six-hourly observations should each be marked by a dot in its appropriate space, and the dots may be afterwards connected by a line.

The temperatures of the dew-point, or of the wet-bulb thermometer, or the mean temperature, may be compared with this primary result by projecting their curves in a similar way beneath it; and should the observations of these points be less frequent than four times in the day, the daily spaces may easily be divided accordingly.

The right-hand compartment is appropriated to the projection of curves of pressure, and the four daily observations of the barometer are to be marked by dots towards the upper part of the scale of inches, and afterwards connected by a line. Towards the lower part of the scale the elastic force of the vapour is to be noted, and the marks to be similarly connected by a line.

On either the scale of temperature or of pressure, occasional comparisons may be made with results obtained at other stations, which, if judiciously selected, cannot fail to prove of high interest and importance. They should, however, be laid down in pencil, or marked by a fainter line.

At the bottom of the first skeleton form will be found a space prepared for the 24 hourly observations of the *twenty-first day* of the month, both in their uncorrected and their corrected state. It is divided into four compartments for 6 hours each. The instruments which can with most facility be observed in this manner, are the barometer with its attached thermometer, and the dry- and wet-bulb thermometers; and columns are appropriated to each of these. It is desirable that the means of each 6 hours should be calculated, and spaces have been provided accordingly for the arithmetical operations.

In casting up the sums and calculating the *means*, care should be taken in all cases to verify the results by repetition; and the Council recommend in every instance, before adding up the columns, to look down each to see that no obvious error of entry (as of an inch in the barometer, a very common error) may remain to vitiate the mean result. The precaution should also be taken of counting the days in each column, so as to make no mistake in the divisor.

The skeleton forms will be interleaved with blank pages, to facilitate computations and comparisons, and to afford space for other observations of atmospheric phenomena, which will perpetually present themselves to those who make it their business or their pleasure to watch the changes of the weather on a judicious plan. The Council, indeed, wish it to be understood, that, in the suggestions which they have offered, they have taken into consideration only such observations as are indispensable for laying the first foundations of meteorological science; some investigations of a more refined character they may, probably, make the subject of a future report.

As soon as the register of a month's observations has been computed, it should be copied, and the copy carefully compared with the original by two persons, one reading aloud from the original, and the other attending to the copy, and then exchanging parts,—a process always advisable whenever great masses of figures are required to be correctly copied.

A copy so verified should be transmitted regularly to such person or public body, as, under the circumstances, may be authorized or best adapted to receive and discuss the observations.

TABLES REFERRED TO IN THE SECTION ENTITLED "INSTRUCTIONS FOR MAKING METEOROLOGICAL "OBSERVATIONS."

TABLE I.

Correction to be added to Barometers for Capillary Action.

Diameter of Tube.	Correction for	
	Unboiled Tubes.	Boiled Tubes.
inch.	inch.	inch.
0·60	0·004	0·002
0·50	0·007	0·003
0·45	0·010	0·005
0·40	0·014	0·007
0·35	0·020	0·010
0·30	0·028	0·014
0·25	0·040	0·020
0·20	0·060	0·029
0·15	0·088	0·044
0·10	0·142	0·070

TABLE II.

Correction to be applied to Barometers with *brass scales*, extending the observation

Temp.	Inches.								Temp.
	24	24·5	25	25·5	26	26·5	27	27·5	
°	+	+	+	+	+	+	+	+	°
0	·061	·063	·064	·065	·067	·068	·069	·071	0
1	·059	·061	·062	·063	·064	·065	·067	·068	1
2	·057	·058	·060	·061	·062	·063	·064	·066	2
3	·055	·056	·057	·059	·060	·061	·062	·063	3
4	·053	·054	·055	·056	·057	·058	·059	·061	4
5	·051	·052	·053	·054	·055	·056	·057	·058	5
6	·049	·050	·051	·052	·053	·054	·055	·056	6
7	·046	·047	·048	·049	·050	·051	·052	·053	7
8	·044	·045	·046	·047	·048	·049	·050	·051	8
9	·042	·043	·044	·045	·046	·046	·047	·048	9
10	·040	·041	·042	·042	·043	·044	·045	·046	10
11	·038	·039	·039	·040	·041	·042	·042	·043	11
12	·036	·036	·037	·038	·039	·039	·040	·041	12
13	·033	·034	·035	·036	·036	·037	·038	·038	13
14	·031	·032	·033	·033	·034	·035	·035	·036	14
15	·029	·030	·030	·031	·032	·032	·033	·033	15
16	·027	·028	·028	·029	·029	·030	·030	·031	16
17	·025	·025	·026	·026	·027	·027	·028	·028	17
18	·023	·023	·024	·024	·025	·025	·025	·026	18
19	·021	·021	·021	·022	·022	·023	·023	·024	19
20	·018	·019	·019	·020	·020	·020	·021	·021	20
21	·016	·017	·017	·017	·018	·018	·018	·019	21
22	·014	·014	·015	·015	·015	·016	·016	·016	22
23	·012	·012	·012	·013	·013	·013	·013	·014	23
24	·010	·010	·010	·010	·011	·011	·011	·011	24
25	·008	·008	·008	·008	·008	·008	·009	·009	25
26	·005	·006	·006	·006	·006	·006	·006	·006	26
27	·003	·003	·003	·003	·004	·004	·004	·004	27
28	·001	·001	·001	·001	·001	·001	·001	·001	28
	−	−	−	−	−	−	−	−	
29	·001	·001	·001	·001	·001	·001	·001	001	29
30	·003	·003	·003	·004	·004	·004	·004	·004	30
31	·005	·006	·006	·006	·006	·006	·006	·006	31
32	·008	·008	·008	·008	·008	·008	·008	·009	32
33	·010	·010	·010	·010	·011	·011	·011	·011	33
34	·012	·012	·012	·013	·013	·013	·013	·014	34
35	·014	·014	·015	·015	·015	·015	·016	·016	35
36	·016	·017	·017	·017	·017	·018	·018	·019	36
37	·018	·019	·019	·019	·020	·020	·021	·021	37
38	·020	·021	·021	·022	·022	·023	·023	·023	38
39	·023	·023	·024	·024	·024	·025	·025	·026	39
40	·025	·025	·026	·026	·027	·027	·028	·028	40
41	·027	·027	·028	·029	·029	·030	·030	·031	41
42	·029	·030	·030	·031	·031	·032	·033	·033	42
43	·031	·032	·032	·033	·034	·034	·035	·036	43
44	·033	·034	·035	·035	·035	·037	·037	·038	44
45	·035	·036	·037	·038	·038	·039	·040	·041	45
46	·038	·038	·039	·040	·041	·042	·042	·043	46
47	·040	·041	·041	·042	·043	·044	·045	·046	47
48	·042	·043	·044	·045	·045	·046	·047	·048	48
49	·044	·045	·046	·047	·048	·049	·050	·050	49
50	·046	·047	·048	·049	·050	·051	·052	·053	50

TABLE II.

from the cistern to the top of the mercurial column, to reduce to 32° Fahrenheit.

Temp.	Inches.							Temp.
	28	28·5	29	29·5	30	30·5	31	
	+	+	+	+	+	+	+	
0	·072	·073	·074	·076	·077	·078	·080	0
1	·069	·071	·072	·073	·074	·076	·077	1
2	·067	·068	·069	·070	·072	·073	·074	2
3	·064	·065	·067	·068	·069	·070	·071	3
4	·062	·063	·064	·065	·066	·067	·068	4
5	·059	·060	·061	·062	·063	·065	·066	5
6	·057	·058	·059	·060	·061	·062	·063	6
7	·054	·055	·056	·057	·058	·059	·060	7
8	·052	·053	·054	·054	·055	·056	·057	8
9	·049	·050	·051	·052	·053	·054	·054	9
10	·047	·047	·048	·049	·050	·051	·052	10
11	·044	·045	·046	·046	·047	·048	·049	11
12	·042	·042	·043	·044	·045	·045	·046	12
13	·039	·040	·040	·041	·042	·043	·043	13
14	·037	·037	·038	·038	·039	·040	·040	14
15	·034	·035	·035	·036	·036	·037	·038	15
16	·032	·032	·033	·033	·034	·034	·035	16
17	·029	·030	·030	·031	·031	·032	·032	17
18	·026	·027	·027	·028	·028	·029	·029	18
19	·024	·024	·025	·025	·026	·026	·027	19
20	·021	·022	·022	·023	·023	·023	·024	20
21	·019	·019	·020	·020	·020	·021	·021	21
22	·016	·017	·017	·017	·018	·018	·018	22
23	·014	·014	·014	·015	·015	·015	·015	23
24	·011	·012	·012	·012	·012	·012	·013	24
25	·009	·009	·009	·009	·009	·010	·010	25
26	·006	·006	·007	·007	·007	·007	·007	26
27	·004	·004	·004	·004	·004	·004	·004	27
28	·001	·001	·001	·001	·001	·001	·001	28
	−	−	−	−	−	−	−	
29	·001	·001	·001	·001	·001	·001	·001	29
30	·004	·004	·004	·004	·004	·004	·004	30
31	·006	·006	·007	·007	·007	·007	·007	31
32	·009	·009	·009	·009	·009	·010	·010	32
33	·011	·012	·012	·012	·012	·012	·012	33
34	·014	·014	·014	·015	·015	·015	·015	34
35	·016	·017	·017	·017	·018	·018	·018	35
36	·019	·019	·020	·020	·020	·021	·021	36
37	·021	·022	·022	·022	·023	·023	·024	37
38	·024	·024	·025	·025	·026	·026	·026	38
39	·026	·027	·027	·028	·028	·029	·029	39
40	·029	·029	·030	·030	·031	·031	·032	40
41	·031	·032	·033	·033	·034	·034	·035	41
42	·034	·034	·035	·036	·036	·037	·037	42
43	·036	·037	·038	·038	·039	·040	·040	43
44	·039	·040	·040	·041	·042	·042	·043	44
45	·041	·042	·043	·044	·044	·045	·046	45
46	·044	·045	·045	·046	·047	·048	·049	46
47	·046	·047	·048	·049	·050	·151	·051	47
48	·049	·050	·051	·052	·052	·053	·054	48
49	·051	·052	·053	·054	·055	·056	·057	49
50	·054	·055	·056	·057	·058	·059	·060	50

TABLE II. (continued.)

Temp.	Inches.								Temp.
	24	24·5	25	25·5	26	26·5	27	27·5	
51°	·048	·049	·050	·051	·052	·053	·054	·055	51°
52	·050	·052	·053	·054	·055	·056	·057	·058	52
53	·053	·054	·055	·056	·057	·058	·059	·060	53
54	·055	·056	·057	·058	·059	·060	·062	·063	54
55	·057	·058	·059	·060	·062	·063	·064	·065	55
56	·059	·060	·061	·063	·064	·065	·066	·068	56
57	·061	·062	·064	·065	·066	·068	·069	·070	57
58	·063	·065	·066	·067	·069	·070	·071	·073	58
59	·065	·067	·068	·070	·071	·072	·074	·075	59
60	·068	·069	·070	·072	·073	·075	·076	·077	60
61	·070	·071	·073	·074	·075	·077	·078	·080	61
62	·072	·073	·075	·076	·078	·079	·081	·082	62
63	·074	·076	·077	·079	·080	·082	·083	·085	63
64	·076	·078	·079	·081	·082	·084	·086	·087	64
65	·078	·080	·082	·083	·085	·086	·088	·090	65
66	·080	·082	·084	·085	·087	·089	·090	·092	66
67	·083	·084	·086	·088	·089	·091	·093	·095	67
68	·085	·086	·088	·090	·092	·094	·095	·097	68
69	·087	·089	·090	·092	·094	·096	·098	·100	69
70	·089	·091	·093	·095	·096	·098	·100	·102	70
71	·091	·093	·095	·097	·099	·101	·102	·104	71
72	·093	·095	·097	·099	·101	·103	·105	·107	72
73	·095	·097	·099	·101	·103	·105	·107	·109	73
74	·097	·099	·102	·104	·106	·108	·110	·112	74
75	·100	·102	·104	·106	·108	·110	·112	·114	75
76	·102	·104	·106	·108	·110	·112	·114	·117	76
77	·104	·106	·108	·110	·112	·115	·117	·119	77
78	·106	·108	·110	·113	·115	·117	·119	·122	78
79	·108	·110	·113	·115	·117	·119	·122	·124	79
80	·110	·113	·115	·117	·119	·122	·124	·126	80
81	·112	·115	·117	.119	·122	·124	·126	·129	81
82	·114	·117	·119	·122	·124	·126	·129	·131	82
83	·117	·119	·121	·124	·126	·129	·131	·134	83
84	·119	·121	·124	·126	·129	·131	·134	·136	84
85	·121	·123	·126	·128	·131	·133	·136	·139	85
86	·123	·126	·128	·131	·133	·136	·138	·141	86
87	·125	·128	·130	·133	·136	·138	·141	·143	87
88	·127	·130	·133	·135	·138	·141	·143	·146	88
89	·129	·132	·135	·137	·140	·143	·146	·148	89
90	·131	·134	·137	·140	·142	·145	·148	·151	90
91	·134	·136	·139	·142	·145	·148	·150	·153	91
92	·136	·139	·141	·144	·147	·150	·153	·156	92
93	·138	·141	·144	·147	·149	·152	·155	·158	93
94	·140	·143	·146	·149	·152	·155	·157	·161	94
95	·142	·145	·148	·151	·154	·157	·160	·163	95
96	·144	·147	·150	·153	·156	·159	·162	·165	96
97	·146	·149	·152	·156	·159	·162	·165	·168	97
98	·148	·152	·155	·158	·161	·164	·167	·170	98
99	·151	·154	·157	·160	·163	·166	·169	·173	99
100	·153	·156	·159	·162	·165	·169	·172	·175	100

TABLE II. (continued).

Temp.	Inches.							Temp.
	28	28·5	29	29·5	30	30·5	31	
51°	·056	·057	·038	·059	·060	·061	·062	51°
52	·059	·060	·061	·062	·063	·064	·065	52
53	·061	·063	·064	·065	·066	·067	·068	53
54	·064	·065	·066	·067	·068	·070	·071	54
55	·066	·068	·069	·070	·071	·072	·073	55
56	·069	·070	·071	·073	·074	·075	·076	56
57	·071	·073	·074	·075	·076	·078	·079	57
58	·074	·075	·077	·078	·079	·081	·082	58
59	·076	·078	·079	·080	·082	·083	·085	59
60	·079	·080	·082	·083	·085	·086	·087	60
61	·081	·083	·084	·086	·087	·089	·090	61
62	·084	·085	·087	·088	·090	·091	·093	62
63	·086	·088	·089	·091	·093	·094	·096	63
64	·089	·090	·092	·094	·095	·097	·098	64
65	·091	·093	·095	·096	·098	·100	·101	65
66	·094	·096	·097	·099	·101	·102	·104	66
67	·096	·098	·100	·102	·103	·105	·107	67
68	·099	·101	·102	·104	·106	·108	·109	68
69	·101	·103	·105	·107	·109	·110	·112	69
70	·104	·106	·108	·109	·111	·113	·115	70
71	·106	·108	·110	·112	·114	·116	·118	71
72	·109	·111	·113	·115	·117	·119	·120	72
73	·111	·113	·115	·117	·119	·121	·123	73
74	·114	·116	·118	·120	·122	·124	·126	74
75	·116	·118	·120	·122	·125	·127	·129	75
76	·119	·121	·123	·125	·127	·129	·131	76
77	·121	·123	·126	·128	·130	·132	·134	77
78	·124	·126	·128	·130	·133	·135	·137	78
79	·126	·128	·131	·133	·135	·137	·140	79
80	·129	·131	·133	·136	·138	·140	·143	80
81	·131	·134	·136	·138	·141	·143	·145	81
82	·134	·136	·138	·141	·143	·146	·148	82
83	·136	·139	·141	·143	·146	·148	·151	83
84	·139	·141	·144	·146	·149	·151	·154	84
85	·141	·144	·146	·149	·151	·154	·156	85
86	·144	·146	·149	·151	·154	·156	·159	86
87	·146	·149	·151	·154	·157	·159	·162	87
88	·149	·151	·154	·157	·159	·162	·165	88
89	·151	·154	·156	·159	·162	·165	·167	89
90	·153	·156	·159	·162	·164	·167	·170	90
91	·156	·159	·162	·165	·167	·170	·173	91
92	·158	·161	·164	·167	·170	·172	·175	92
93	·161	·164	·167	·170	·172	·175	·178	93
94	·163	·166	·169	·172	·175	·177	·180	94
95	·166	·169	·172	·175	·178	·180	·183	95
96	·168	·171	·174	·178	·181	·183	·186	96
97	·171	·174	·177	·180	·183	·186	·189	97
98	·173	·176	·179	·183	·186	·188	·191	98
99	·176	·179	·182	·185	·188	·191	·194	99
100	·178	·181	·184	·188	·191	·194	·197	100

Table III.

Correction to be applied to Barometers, the scales of which are engraven on *glass*, to reduce the observations to 32° Fahrenheit.

Temp.	Inches. 28·0	Inches. 28·5	Inches. 29·0	Inches. 29·5	Inches. 30·0	Inches. 30·5	Inches. 31·0	Inches. 31·5
25	+·017	+·017	+·017	+·018	+·018	+·018	+·019	+·019
30	+·005	+·005	+·005	+·005	+·005	+·005	+·005	+·005
35	—·007	—·007	—·007	—·008	—·008	—·008	—·008	—·008
40	—·019	—·020	—·020	—·020	—·021	—·021	—·021	—·022
45	—·031	—·032	—·032	—·033	—·033	—·034	—·035	—·036
50	—·043	—·044	—·045	—·046	—·046	—·047	—·048	—·049
55	—·055	—·056	—·057	—·058	—·059	—·060	—·061	—·062
60	—·067	—·068	—·069	—·071	—·072	—·074	—·075	—·076
65	—·079	—·081	—·082	—·083	—·085	—·086	—·088	—·089
70	—·091	—·093	—·094	—·096	—·098	—·100	—·101	—·103
75	—·103	—·105	—·106	—·109	—·111	—·114	—·116	—·118

Table IV.

Showing the force of the wind on a square foot for different heights of the Column of Water in Lind's Wind-gauge.

Height of the Column of Water.	Force of the Wind in Avoirdupois Pounds.	Common designation of such a wind.
inches.		
12	62·5	
11	57·29	
10	52·08	Most violent hurricane.
9	46·87	
8	44·66	A very great hurricane.
7	36·55	A great hurricane.
6	31·75	A hurricane.
5	26·04	A very great storm.
4	20·83	A great storm.
3	15·62	A storm.
2	10·42	A very high wind.
1	5·21	A high wind.
0·5	2·60	A brisk gale.
0·1.	0·52	A fresh breeze.
0·05	0·26	A pleasant wind.

In great degrees of cold, a saturated solution of sea salt may be used instead of water, the specific gravity of which is 1·244. If the force in the above Table for any height be multiplied by the specific gravity, the product will be the true force, as measured by the solution.

TABLE V.

Elastic Force of Aqueous Vapour for every degree of temperature, from 0° to 103° Fahr.

Temp. Fahr.	Force. Inches of Mercury.	Temp. Fahr.	Force. Inches of Mercury.	Temp. Fahr.	Force. Inches of Mercury.	Temp. Fahr.	Force. Inches of Mercury.
0°	0·051	32°	0·186	63°	0 570	94°	1·562
1	0·053	33	0·193	64	0·590	95	1·610
2	0·056	34	0·200	65	0·611	96	1·660
3	0·058	35	0·208	66	0·632	97	1·712
4	0·060	30	0·216	67	0·654	98	1·764
5	0·063	37	0·224	68	0·676	99	1·819
6	0·066	38	0·233	69	0·699	100	1·874
7	0·069	39	0·242	70	0·723	101	1·931
8	0·071	40	0·251	71	0·748	102	1·990
9	0·074	41	0·260	72	0·773	103	2·050
10	0·078	42	0·270	73	0·799	104	2·112
11	0·081	43	0·280	74	0·826	105	2·176
12	0·084	44	0·291	75	0·854	106	2·241
13	0·088	45	0·302	76	0·882	107	2·307
14	0·092	46	0·313	77	0·911	108	2·376
15	0·095	47	0·324	78	0·942	109	2·447
16	0·099	48	0·336	79	0·973	110	2·519
17	0·103	49	0·349	80	1·005	111	2·593
18	0·107	50	0·361	81	1·036	112	2·669
19	0·112	51	0·375	82	1·072	113	2·747
20	0·116	52	0·389	83	1·106	114	2·826
21	0·121	53	0·402	84	1·142	115	2·908
22	0·126	54	0·417	85	1·179	116	2·992
23	0·131	55	0·432	86	1·217	117	3·078
24	0·136	56	0·447	87	1·256	118	3·166
25	0·142	57	0·463	88	1·296	119	3·257
26	0·147	58	0·480	89	1·337	120	3·349
27	0·153	59	0·497	90	1·380	121	3·444
28	0·159	60	0·514	91	1·423	122	3·542
29	0·165	61	0·532	92	1·468	123	3·641
30	0·172	62	0·551	93	1·514	124	3·743
31	0·179						

Temp.	Inches.							
	20	20·5	21	21·5	22	22·5	23	23·5
	+	+	+	+	+	+	+	+
0	·051	·053	·054	·055	·056	·058	·059	·060
1	·049	·051	·052	·053	·054	·056	·057	·058
2	·048	·049	·050	·051	·052	·054	·055	·056
3	·046	·047	·048	·049	·050	·052	·053	·054
4	·044	·045	·046	·047	·048	·050	·051	·052
5	·042	·043	·044	·045	·046	·048	·049	·050
6	·040	·042	·042	·044	·044	·046	·047	·048
7	·039	·040	·041	·042	·042	·044	·044	·046
8	·037	·038	·039	·040	·041	·041	·042	·043
9	·035	·036	·037	·038	·039	·039	·040	·041
10	·033	·034	·035	·036	·037	·037	·038	·039
11	·031	·032	·033	·034	·035	·035	·036	·037
12	·030	·030	·031	·032	·033	·033	·034	·035
13	·028	·029	·029	·030	·031	·031	·032	·033
14	·026	·027	·027	·028	·029	·029	·030	·031
15	·024	·025	·026	·026	·027	·027	·028	·029
16	·022	·023	·024	·024	·025	·025	·026	·026
17	·021	·021	·022	·022	·023	·023	·024	·024
18	·019	·019	·020	·020	·021	·021	·022	·022
19	·017	·018	·018	·018	·019	·019	·020	·020
20	·015	·016	·016	·016	·017	·017	·018	·018
21	·014	·014	·014	·015	·015	·015	·015	·016
22	·012	·012	·012	·013	·013	·013	·013	·014
23	·010	·010	·010	·011	·011	·011	·011	·012
24	·008	·008	·009	·009	·009	·009	·009	·010
25	·006	·007	·007	·007	·007	·007	·007	·007
26	·005	·005	·005	·005	·005	·005	·005	·005
27	·003	·003	·003	·003	·003	·003	·003	·003
28	·001	·001	·001	·001	·001	·001	·001	·001
	−	−	−	−	−	−	−	−
29	·001	·001	·001	·001	·001	·001	·001	·001
30	·003	·003	·003	·003	·003	·003	·003	·003
31	·005	·005	·005	·005	·005	·005	·005	·005
32	·006	·006	·007	·007	·007	·007	·007	·007
33	·008	·008	·008	·009	·009	·009	·009	·010
34	·010	·010	·010	·011	·011	·011	·011	·012
35	·012	·012	·012	·013	·013	·013	·013	·014
36	·013	·014	·014	·014	·015	·015	·016	·016
37	·015	·016	·016	·016	·017	·017	·018	·018
38	·017	·017	·018	·018	·019	·019	·020	·020
39	·019	·019	·020	·020	·021	·021	·022	·022
40	·021	·021	·022	·022	·023	·023	·024	·024
41	·022	·023	·024	·024	·025	·025	·026	·026
42	·024	·025	·025	·026	·027	·027	·028	·028
43	·026	·027	·027	·028	·029	·029	·030	·031
44	·028	·029	·029	·030	·031	·031	·032	·033
45	·030	·030	·031	·032	·033	·033	·034	·033
46	·031	·032	·033	·034	·035	·035	·036	·035
47	·033	·034	·035	·036	·036	·037	·038	·037
48	·035	·036	·037	·038	·038	·039	·040	·039
49	·037	·038	·039	·040	·040	·041	·042	·041
50	·038	·039	·040	·041	·042	·043	·044	·045

101

PHYSICAL REPORT (continued).

Temp.	Inches.							
	20	20·5	21	21·5	22	22·5	23	23·5
51	·040	·041	·042	·043	·044	·045	·046	·047
52	·042	·043	·044	·045	·046	·047	·048	·049
53	·044	·045	·046	·047	·048	·049	·050	·052
54	·046	·047	·048	·049	·050	·051	·052	·054
55	·047	·049	·050	·051	·052	·053	·055	·056
56	·049	·050	·052	·053	·054	·055	·057	·058
57	·051	·052	·054	·055	·056	·057	·059	·060
58	·053	·054	·055	·057	·058	·059	·061	·062
59	·055	·056	·057	·059	·060	·061	·063	·064
60	·056	·058	·059	·061	·062	·063	·065	·066
61	·058	·060	·061	·062	·064	·065	·067	·068
62	·060	·061	·063	·064	·066	·067	·069	·070
63	·062	·063	·065	·066	·068	·069	·071	·072
64	·063	·065	·067	·068	·070	·071	·073	·075
65	·065	·067	·068	·070	·072	·073	·075	·077
66	·067	·069	·070	·072	·074	·075	·077	·079
67	·069	·071	·072	·074	·076	·077	·079	·081
68	·071	·072	·074	·076	·078	·079	·081	·083
69	·072	·074	·076	·078	·080	·081	·083	·085
70	·074	·076	·078	·080	·082	·083	·085	·087
71	·076	·078	·080	·082	·083	·085	·087	·089
72	·078	·080	·082	·084	·085	·087	·089	·091
73	·079	·081	·083	·085	·087	·089	·091	·093
74	·081	·083	·085	·087	·089	·091	·093	·095
75	·083	·085	·087	·089	·091	·093	·095	·098
76	·085	·087	·089	·091	·093	·095	·097	·100
77	·087	·089	·091	·093	·095	·097	·100	·102
78	·088	·091	·093	·095	·097	·099	·102	·104
79	·090	·092	·095	·097	·099	·101	·104	·106
80	·092	·094	·096	·099	·101	·103	·106	·108
81	·094	·096	·098	·101	·103	·105	·108	·110
82	·095	·098	·100	·103	·105	·107	·110	·112
83	·097	·100	·102	·104	·107	·109	·112	·114
84	·099	·101	·104	·106	·109	·111	·114	·116
85	·101	·103	·106	·108	·111	·113	·116	·118
86	·103	·105	·108	·110	·113	·115	·118	·120
87	·104	·107	·109	·112	·115	·117	·120	·123
88	·106	·109	·111	·114	·117	·119	·122	·125
89	·108	·111	·113	·116	·119	·121	·124	·127
90	·110	·112	·115	·118	·121	·123	·126	·129
91	·111	·114	·117	·120	·122	·125	·128	·131
92	·113	·116	·119	·122	·124	·127	·130	·133
93	·115	·118	·121	·124	·126	·129	·132	·135
94	·117	·120	·122	·125	·128	·131	·134	·137
95	·118	·121	·124	·127	·130	·133	·136	·139
96	·120	·123	·126	·129	·132	·135	·138	·141
97	·122	·125	·128	·131	·134	·137	·140	·143
98	·124	·127	·130	·133	·136	·139	·142	·145
99	·125	·129	·132	·135	·138	·141	·144	·147
100	·127	·130	·134	·137	·140	·143	·146	·150

APPENDIX A.

The following letters from Baron Von Humboldt to the Earl of Minto, and from Pofessor Erman to Major Sabine, having been communicated to the Royal Society, the President and Council have deemed it desirable that they should form a part of this publication, with the permission of the respective parties.

Letter from the Baron Alexander von Humboldt to the Earl of Minto.

MILORD:

Berlin, ce 12 Oct., 1839.

LORSQ'AU printems de l'année 1836, j'adressai une lettre à S. A. R. Mgr. le Duc de Sussex sur les moyens propres à perfectionner la connoissance du magnétisme terrestre par l'établissement de *stations magnétiques et d'observations correspondantes*, je sollicitai le concours puissant de la Société Royale de Londres en faveur de travaux qui, émanant à la fois de plusieurs grands centres scientifiques de l'Europe, pourroient conduire progressivement à la connoissance précise des lois de la nature. Ma démarche fut accueillie avec bienveillance, et la Société Royale daigna recommander à la protection spéciale du Gouvernement de Sa Majesté l'établissement de plusieurs stations permanentes dans les régions tropicales, et dans les parties tempérées de l'hémisphère austral.

Cette protection du Gouvernement a été accordée avec une munificence qui dépasse de bien loin l'espoir des hommes le plus ardemment occupés des variations du magnétisme terrestre, selon les trois coordonnées de déclinaison, d'inclinaison, et d'intensité absolue. Ce ne sont pas seulement des stations magnétiques qui seront fondées dans les lieux les plus propres à la manifestation des changemens que subit la distribution des forces; c'est une grande *expédition antarctique* qui a été ordonnée sous le commandement d'un savant et intrépide navigateur, le Capitaine James Clark Ross; expédition qui embrassera dans des travaux sagement preparés tous les problêmes du magnétisme terrestre, de la configuration du globe, de la distribution de la chaleur, du mouvement des eaux de l'océan, de la constitution géologique du sol, de la géographie des plantes et des animaux.

Je crois remplir un devoir sacré en offrant au Premier Lord de l'Amirauté, à Monsieur le Comte de Minto, l'hommage respectueux de la plus vive reconnoissance dont sont pénétrés tous ceux qui cultivent les sciences, et leur ont voué une vie laborieuse. Cette reconnoissance est due au Ministre qui, dans des vues élevées et si favorables aux progrès de l'intelligence, a réalisé l'exécution du voyage antarctique. La bienveillance personnelle dont votre Excellence m a honoré, pendant Son séjour à Paris et à la Cour de mon Souverain, me donne le courage de Lui communiquer en même·tems quelques considérations qui se rattachent au but principal d'une vaste et noble entreprise. Ma franchise ne sera pas mal interprétée.

La *variabilité* des phénomènes est ce qui caractérise le plus le magnétisme terrestre : variabilité selon une marche lente et périodique, quelquefois intermittente aussi, comme effet de perturbations brusques et instantanées. Il en résulte que pour approfondir les lois du magnétisme terrestre, il est d'une haute importance de connoître l'état magnétique du Globe à une même époque donnée : ou, du moins, selon des observations faites à des époques très rapprochées. Il y a presque déjà trente ans que, dans le *Recueil* de mes *Observations astronomiques*, j'ai indiqué combien il serait précieux pour la Physique du globe, si plusieurs bâtimens munis d'excellens instrumens, parcouraient simultanément l'équateur magnétique et les lignes sans déclinaison, pour fixer à la même époque dans le vaste bassin des mers, la déclinaison, l'inclinaison, et l'intensité des forces magnétiques. J'insistai aussi, (malgré l'imperfection des instrumens et des méthodes d'alors,) d'après ma propre expérience, sur la possibilité de déterminer sur mer, et avec une précision suffisante, les variations de ces deux derniers élémens. (Rel. hist. T. 1. p. 262.) Je montrai combien ces déterminations océaniques sembloient offrir d'avantages, là, où les couches d'eau sont assez épaisses pour que l'on ait moins à craindre les perturbations locales dues à la constitution minéralogique du fond.

Guidé par des considérations analogues, j'ose exprimer le désir, que pour rendre plus fructueux encore l'immense travail qui sera exécuté en trois années, soit par l'expédition du Capitaine Ross, soit dans les nombreuses stations magnétiques répandues sur la surface des continens et des iles, Votre Excellence voulût bien ordonner simultanément quelques expéditions partielles et supplémentaires. Deux savans, auxquels nous devons des travaux importans sur la connoissance des variations du magnétisme terrestre, M. le Major Sabine et M. Lloyd, professeur à Dublin, m'ont déjà donné l'heureuse nouvelle que le Gouvernement de Sa Majesté enverroit à Otaheité, à cette métropole de l'Océan pacifique, illustrée par d'anciens travaux astronomiques, un officier très-instruit et muni d'appareils magnétiques. Le grand nombre de bâtimens de la marine royale qui se trouvent le plus souvent en station sur les côtes occidentales de l'Amérique du sud, et dans les mers de l'Inde, faciliteront peut-être les moyens de multiplier les investigations que j'appelle *supplementaires*, et dont, pour le moment, le but principal seroit la connoissance expérimentale de l'équateur magnétique, et des lignes sans déclinaison.

I. Un bâtiment muni d'instrumens propres à mesurer l'inclinaison, la déclinaison, et l'intensité, pourroit, en partant des côtes du Pérou, suivre l'équateur magnétique, ou la courbe d'inclinaison zéro, jusqu aux côtes de la péninsule de Malacca, et, si le vent le permet, jusqu'au détroit de Bab-el-Mandel. Un second bâtiment pourroit parcourir l'équateur magnétique depuis le Golfe de Guinée jusqu'aux côtes du Brésil. On détermineroit avec une grande précision astronomique les points du littoral où la courbe d'inclinaison zéro qui n'est pas un grand cercle de la Sphère, coupe les continens et les iles : on apprendroit à connoître les changemens de sinuosité et les mouvemens des *nœuds* (points d'intersection des équateurs magnétique et terrestre) qui ont eu lieu depuis les époques des voyages antérieurs. Comme les lignes isodynamiques et isoclines ne sont aucunement parallèles, il seroit à désirer que les intensités fussent aussi déterminées le long de l'équateur magnétique, ou dans la proximité la plus immédiate.

II. Quant aux parties des lignes sans déclinaison qui deviennent accessibles aux navigateurs, j'oserai, Monsieur le Comte, les indiquer toutes, non dans le vain espoir que des observations simultanées puissent les embrasser dans leur ensemble pendant la durée du séjour du Capt. Ross dans les hautes régions antarctiques, mais seulement pour faciliter le choix à Votre Excellence selon les combinaisons fortuites que peuvent offrir des traverseés ou des stations éphémères de bâtimens de la marine royale. Je n' ignore pas que d'après les grandes vues sur les véritables fondemens d'une *Théorie générale du magnétisme terrestre* qui sont dues à M. Gauss, soit la connoissance approfondie de l'intensité horizontale, soit la multiplicité et la sage répartition des points dans lesquels les trois élémens de déclinaison d'inclinaison et d'intensité ont éte simultanément mesurés, pour trouver la valeur de V (§. 4 et 27), et par conséquent aussi de $\frac{V}{R}$, sont les points vitaux du problême qu'a résolu l'illustre Géomètre : mais les besoins actuels du Pilotage, les corrections habituelles du rumb, et des chemins parcourus, donnent encore une importance speciale et *pratique* à l'élément de la déclinaison. On apprécieroit une détermination expérimentale, *c. a. d.* par observation immédiate, avant que l'édifice théorique ait pu être complété et terminé dans son ensemble ; on l'apprécieroit d'autant plus que les lignes isogones ont un mouvement très-inégal dans les différentes portions de leurs traces, et que l'action combinée des *petites attractions magnétiques locales* cause des déviations partielles de la direction moyenne des lignes d'égale déclinaison, déviations qui intéressent la sécurité des routes, et qui resteront long-temps hors de l'atteinte de la théorie générale la plus solidement établie. Je signale ici de préférence la direction des lignes sans déclinaison, auxquelles des considérations de *Géographie physique* doivent conserver une partie de leur ancienne importance.

(*a.*) L'expédition antarctique, en arrivant par l'ouest de la Terre Kerguelen à celle de Van Diemen, aura traversé la ligne sans déclinaison qui remonte au nord vers la Terre de Nuyts (Australie.) Il seroit important de fixer astronomiquement, comme je l'ai fait observer pour l'équateur magnétique, les points méridionaux et septentrionaux du littoral de la Nouvelle Hollande, où la ligne de déclinaison zéro traverse le continent australien, et de poursuivre cette courbe, d'abord vers l' O. N. O , et ensuite vers le nord, depuis la Baie de Vansittart, ou le Cap Bougainville, jusq' aux iles Maldives, et les attérages de Surate dans l'Inde. Les connoissances acquises par les beaux travaux de Hansteen, d'Adolphe Erman et de George Fuss sur la grande sinuosité des lignes isogones de la Sibérie rend très-difficile de se former aujourd'hui une idée exacte de la liaison de ces lignes avec les lignes correspondantes dans les Mers de l'Inde et de la Chine D'après les cartes intéressantes qui accompagnent l'exposé de la *Théorie générale* par M. Gauss, la ligne de déclinaison zéro ne coupe le continent asiatique que près de l'entrée du Golfe Persique : elle remonte directement de là vers le nord à la Mer Caspienne et à la Mer Blanche. D'après M. Barlow elle se replie du Golfe de Cambaye vers le N.E. et reparoît dans les Mers de la Chine et du Japon, entre l'extrémité septentrionale de l'Ile Formose et la péninsule Seghalienne.

Ce seroit jeter une vive lumière sur un des points les plus obscurs du magnétisme terrestre que de lever les doutes qui enveloppent le prolongement de cette ligne de déclinaison zéro de la mer des Indes, et de faire connoître par des observations précises la direction et la distribution des forces à l'ouest de l'Indus entre Candahar, Balkh, Kundouz et le Pnndjab (la Pentapotamie). Il est probable que la marche victorieuse des armées de S. M. vers Caboul, et le séjour des troupes dans l'Afghanistan pourront donner lieu à des recherches de ce genre, au moyen des petits appareils magnétiques que l'on destine pour l'Inde. Il resteroit à examiner pour la même époque la position de la ligne zéro dans les mers du Japon au nord de l'Isle Formose, comme dans l'Océan Glacial dans la partie très-accessible entre Spitzbergen et la Mer Blanche.

Suivre les traces de l'équateur magnétique, ou celles des lignes sans léclinaison, c'est gouverner (diriger la route du vaisseau) de manière à couper les lignes zéro dans les intervalles les plus petits, en changeant de rumb chaque fois que les observations d'inclinaison ou de déclinaison prouvent qu'on a dévié.

(*b.*) Si du système oriental, ou de l'ancien continent, nous passons au système magnétique americain et atlantique, nous aurions à désirer la détermination simultanée des portions de la ligne sans déclinaison qui remonte à l'est de la Géorgie du sud vers St. Salvador du Brésil, quitte le continent près de Maranham, et se dirige au N. O. vers le Cap Charles et la Baye de Chesapeak. Les mers que traverse cette ligne sont si fréquentées que de nombreuses observations magnétiques y ont été faites, et se trouvent conservées dans les archives du Dépôt de la Marine Royale ; mais il ne suffit pas d'avoir coupé souvent à différentes époques la ligne zéro, il s'agit de la poursuivre, autant que les vents le permettent, dans toute son étendue. Je devrais hésiter, M. le Comte, à faire mention du prolongement le plus boréal de la ligne atlantique à travers le Canada et la Baie d'Hudson, mais je dois considérer la surface du globe dans son ensemble, et fixer l'attention des navigateurs sur les changemens qui peuvent être survenus dans les dernières années.

(c.) La Mer du Sud, si l'on en excepte les côtes du Japon n a de nos jours pas de variation zéro. Le *nœud circulaire qui renferme l'archipel des Marquesas* près du minimum des variations orientales (5°) mérite de nouvelles investigations dont pourroit se charger le bâtiment qui suivrait l'équateur magnétique du Pérou vers l'Inde. La forme de ce nœud circulaire *c. à d.* l'espacement variable des courbes isogones qui le constituent, et le déplacement progressif du nœud entier, sont des phénomènes également remarquables et qui contrastent avec le grand nœud circulaire de l'Asie orientale, auquel, selon le mémoire de M. Gauss, appartient la courbe de déclinaison zéro des mers du Japon et de la Chine.

Je compte sur votre ancienne bienveillance, Milord, en osant vous importuner si longuement de considérations sur l'utilité que pourraient offrir des observations simultanées, par l'emploi d'instrumens et de méthodes semblables, dans les différentes régions des deux hémisphères. J'ai touché aux moyens de compléter les resultats de la grande expédition antarctique, et d'en augmenter la valeur. Votre Excellence jugera dans sa sagesse, de ce qui, parmi tant d'objets importans pour l'*art nautique* et pour la *Géographie physique*, pourra lui paroître d'une exécution facile. Je sais borner mes espérances.

Je supplie V. E. de jetter les yeux sur quelques *additions aux instructions scientifiques* que j'ose Lui adresser. C'est presque être présomptueux que de vouloir ajouter à un excellent travail, rédigé en partie par Sir J. Herschel. J'ai cédé aux instances amicales de MM. Sabine et Lloyd, et je vous supplie, Milord, de vouloir bien faire mettre entre les mains de Sir J. Herschel un écrit fragmentaire dans lequel ce grand astronome et savant physicien effacera librement tout ce qui lui paroîtra peu exact, ou moins digne de l'attention des voyageurs.

Je suis, &c., &c.

A. DE HUMBOLDT.

Additions fragmentaires aux " Instructions for the Scientific Expedition to the Antarctic Regions."

Les personnes qui sont chargées des observations scientifiques, ayant des connoissances très-variées, il suffit de leur rappeler avec la plus grande concision les points qui paroissent de quelque importance dans le cours de leurs travaux.

I. Forme de la Surface Continentale.

Mouvemens des terres par *soulèvement* ou par *dépression*, soit lents et progressifs, soit brusques et instantanés, toujours comme effet de la réaction de l'intérieur fluide d'une planète vers sa croûte plus ou moins consolidée.

Il seroit important de placer des marques sur les côtes des continens et des iles, à une élévation rigoureusement déterminée au dessus des plus hautes marées. Je préférerois des barres de cuivre préparées d'avance en Angleterre, ayant une inscription de la date et le nom du Capitaine Ross. Un trait ou sillon creusé dans le rocher, réuniroit deux marques métalliques eloignées l'une de l'autre au moins de 15 pieds. Le sillon doit être très-exactement horizontal. Pour chaque endroit on aura vérifié l'élévation moyenne des marées d'une manière approximative. Des marques semblables, mais de fer et de 2 pieds de long, ont été placées (à ma prière, après mon retour de Sibérie) par M. Lenz, membre de l'Académie de St. Petersbourg, sur les côtes rocheuses de la Mer Caspienne près de Bazou (voyez Poggendorf, Annalen, t. xxvi. p. 364.). Les barres sont scellées par du plomb fondu.

II. Magnétisme Terrestre.

Tout ce qui a rapport à l'importance de la simultanéité des déterminations d'inclinaison, de déclinaison et d'intensité magnètiques a été consigné dans la lettre que j'ai eu l'honneur d'adresser à M. le Comte de Minto, Premier Lord de l'Amirauté. J'ai rappelé ce qui est relatif à la forme, et aux directions actuelles de l'équateur magnétique (courbe d'inclinaison zéro) et des lignes sans déclinaison. Je n'ajoute ici que le désir que l'on puisse observer en outre des époques prescrites par M. Gauss, aux époques astronomiquement importantes des *solstices* et des *équinoxes*, comme je l'ai fait conjointement avec M. Oltmanns en 1806 et 1807, pendant 5 et 6 jours et autant de nuits. A cause de la plus grande précision des instrumens actuels, 24 ou 36 heures suffiroient. Je signale aussi les points suivans :—Examiner les influences lunaires d'après les indications de M. Kreil, astronome de Milan, aujourd'hui à Prague ; faire attention aux orages, aux grandes chutes de grêle ou de neige, aux jours couverts ou sereins ; voir si des changemens atmosphériques modifient les phénomènes magnétiques d'une manière sensible et stable ; examiner si sur mer ou sur les glaces polaires, on remarque quelque influence de la constitution minéralogique du fond ; si des perturbations locales se font sentir sur mer, là ou l'on peut supposer que les eaux ne sont pas très-profondes. L'intensité des forces se trouvoit diminuée à la hauteur que M. Gay Lussac a atteinte en ballon : on reconnoit cette diminution, lorsqu'on corrige les observations de ce savant par la température des couches d'air qu'il a parcourues. La position dans un vaisseau à la surface des mers est une position semblable ; moins par rapport à la surface moyenne de la terre, que par rapport à l'indépendance relative aux attractions locales. Les observations faites sur de hautes montagnes, au dessus de 2500 toises, (observations d'inclinaison et d'intensité recueillies soit par moi, soit tout récemment par d'autres voyageurs) donnent des résultats peu concordans à cause des perturbations dues aux couches soulevées de la croûte terrestre. Ces considérations sur le décroissement très-lent des forces magnétiques dans le rapport hypsométrique, et sur la petitesse de la profondeur moyenne de l'océan, méritent l'attention des physiciens. Même sur le sol volcanique de Rome, nous n'avons pas trouvé M. Gay Lussac et moi, de différence sensible dans l'intensité de la force horizon-

tale au Monte Pincio à la Villa Borghese et à Tivoli. Ces expériences seront très-aisées à répéter sur la glace, où l'on peut s'éloig
ner à de grandes distances du navire, et où des influences du fond de
la mer, si elles existent, doivent se manifester au milieu de la marche
uniforme des phénomènes d'intensité ou d'inclinaison.

Les tremblemens de terre m'ont paru agir quelquefois sur l'inclinaison. Multiplier les observations d'inclinaison horaire là ou
les secousses sont fréquentes.

Les aurores boréales changent-elles parfois la force horizontale
sans influer sur l'inclinaison? Y a-t-il quelque aspect particulier à
cette classe d'aurores boréales ou australes, qui affectent peu les déclinaisons horaires de l'aiguille?

Observer de préférence les variations magnétiques aux époques
où beaucoup d'étoiles filantes entrent dans l'atmosphère. Examiner
si les grandes perturbations (les orages magnétiques) se répétent
pendant plusieurs jours aux mêmes heures ; si en général ces
orages magnétiques ne sont pas beaucoup plus fréquens de nuit,
lorsque le soleil ne règle et ne tempère plus par son séjour au dessus
de l'horizon la marche de l'aiguille. Il est d'un vif intérêt de dé-
couvrir les rapports du magnétisme terrestre (et de ses manifesta-
tions variables) avec d'autres phénomènes physiques, soit dans les
mouvemens qui dépendent du tems vrai (du passage du soleil par le
méridien de chaque lieu), soit dans les mouvemens isochrones, c. à d.
dans ceux dont on peut déduire la différence de longitude avec un
degré de précision inattendue.

III. Mers.

Observer les différences de température dans la haute et la basse
mer, comme l'influence que la pente plus ou moins rapide des accores
produit sur le refroidissement des bas-fonds ; mesurer la distance à
laquelle les bancs de glace agissent sur la température des eaux de
la surface. Les températures des basses couches de la mer ont ac-
quis un nouvel intérêt depuis que dans le voyage de Kotzebue, M.
Lenz, muni d'excellens instrumens, a trouvé souvent sous les tropiques (par 7° et par 21° de latitude à 600 et 900 toises de profondeur) 2·21 et 2·44 du thermomètre centigrade, (Poggendorf, t. xx.
p. 73,) et que l'on sait que le maximum de densité de l'eau pure
n'est pas applicable à l'eau de mer. Le Capitaine Bérard, avec
une ligne de sonde d'un millimètre de diamètre, est parvenu à
sonder jusqu'à 1334 toises de profondeur (Bérard, *Description
des Côtes d'Alger*, 1837, p. 41). Les thermomètres à minimum et
à maximum de M. Magnus et de M. Walferdin sont d'un emploi
très-précis comme l'ont prouvé les belles expériences de M. Arago
dans les puits artésiens. C'est dans les courans océaniques d'une
haute température que les sondes thermométriques seroient surtout
d'un grand intérêt. Examiner si le courant d'eaux froides qui
longe les côtes du Pérou jusqu'au Cap Pariña, où il dévie vers les
Galapagos, et dans lequel j'ai trouvé par les 12° de latitude sud
l'eau de la surface seulement à 12·4 Réaumur, quand hors du courant, la mer étoit à 22 R., prend sa source 75° à l'ouest du méridien

du Cap Horn par les 60° et 65° de latitude sud. Ce mouvement des eaux froides est il d'abord dirigé vers le nord-nord-est, et puis (sur le parallèle de 35° sud) vers l'ouest, en frappant contre les côtes du Chili, et se divisant sur ces côtes en deux courans vers le nord et le sud? Examiner la température de ce fleuve pélagique loin du littoral à l'ouest du Chili. (Voyez l'intéressante *Carte du mouvement des eaux dans le Grand Océan Austral, par le Capitaine Duperrey*, 1831, et l'Atlas Physique de Berghaus, Cahier I. No. 4.)

Employer différens moyens, ou de nivellement optique le long des mâts, ou de dépression d'horizon (si le soleil est visible), ou de privation du vent par les vagues en mesurant en même tems l'inclinaison de la mâture, pour déterminer, dans une tempète, loin des côtes, le maximum si souvent contesté de la hauteur des vagues. J'ai cru trouver ce maximum par le moyen de la dépression de l'horizon, dans la Mer du Sud, pendant une de ces tempètes désignées sous le nom de Papagayos, à l'ouest des côtes de Guatimala, de 43 pieds français. D autres voyageurs croyent ce resultat de beaucoup trop grand.

IV. Atmosphère.

Si la pression moyenne de l'air au niveau des mers diminue dans l'hémisphère boréal, depuis le parallèle de 55° vers les tropiques et vers l'équateur, elle paroît, par de certaines longitudes, diminuer aussi, entre les 55° et 68°, et puis augmenter de nouveau. D'après les recherches de M. Schouw, on trouve à zéro de température et en appliquant avec M. Poggendorf la correction relative à la pesanteur, pour

	Nord.	Lignes *
Christianborg . . .	$5\frac{1}{2}$° .	Bar. 336·09
La Guayra	10	6·16
Palermo	38	8·00?
Naples . . . . · .	41	7·82
Londres	$51\frac{1}{4}$	7·53
Altona	$53\frac{1}{2}$	7·35
Danzig	$54\frac{1}{2}$	7·24
Edinburgh . . .	56	6·46
Christiania . . .	60	6·74
Bergen.	60	6·02
Reikiavik . . .	64	3·89
Godthaab	64	3·86
Upermaviz . . .	73	5·49
l'Ile Melville . . .	$74\frac{1}{2}$	6·35
Spitzbergen . . .	$75\frac{1}{2}$	6·23

En faisant abstraction de la correction relative à la pesanteur, on auroit, pour La Guayra 336·98, pour Londres 337·33, pour Reikiavik 333·36, pour l'Ile Melville 335·61. (Poggendorf, t. xxvi. p. 241 et 475.) Il est important d'avoir ces chiffres sous les yeux pour les comparer avec les hauteurs moyennes du barometre que

---

* Ancienne mesure de France.

l'on obtiendra, réduites à zéro de température, par différentes latitudes et longitudes de l'hemisphère austral.

On comparera aussi la direction moyenne des vents de l'année et
des saisons avec la pression atmosphérique.

Quant à la direction du *tournoiement* du vent dans les deux hémisphères, effet de la rotation du Globe et de la vitesse des molécules
d'air correspondant à chaque parallèle, je recommande les ingénieuses recherches de M. Dove dans les *Meteorologische Untersu-
chungen*, 1837, pp. 124—138. Déjà Bacon de Verulam a dit, dans
le chapitre *De successione ventorum* : "Si ventus se mutet conformi-
ter ad motum solis, *non* revertitur plerumque." La direction du
tournoiement est opposée dans les deux hémisphères (*Churucca,
Viage al Magellanes*, 1793, p. 15); mais ce fait, connu depuis
long-tems des marins, n'avoit pas été examine sous le rapport de
ces importantes influences météorologiques. Examiner la températures des plages et la comparer à la température de l'air. Placer
des thermomètres dans le sol à différentes profondeurs, sous différentes latitudes.

L'observation des *réfractions* par un froid très-intense seroit surtout très-importante, si par l'ascension à quelque montagne voisine et
d'une élévation considérable, on pouvoit déterminer en même-tems
le décroissement du calorique. Dans le voyage de la corvette *La
Recherche* au Spitzberg et aux côtes de Laponie, on a voulu se
servir de ballons captifs et de thermomètrographes, mais des expériences de ce genre sont d'une exécution peu facile. Le décroissement de la chaleur est si lent pendant de grands abaissemens du
thermomètre, que les observations de réfraction de M. Svanberg
faites en Laponie par 29° centésimaux audessous du point de la con-
gélation donnent, d'après les formules de M. Laplace, un décroissement de 243 mètres par degré centésimal.

L'Ephéméride des étoiles filantes, publiée par M. Quetelet, sera
indispensable aux voyageurs, pour fixer leur attention sur d'autres
jours que ceux d'Aout et de Novembre. Examiner si les jours des
grandes chutes d'étoiles filantes il y a simultanément des traces
d'aurores australes. L'Amiral Wrangel assure avoir observé souvent, dans son expédition aux iles des Ours et de Kolioutchin dans
la Mer glaciale, que pendant les aurores boréales, certaines régions
du ciel ne sont devenues lumineuses que lorsque des étoiles filantes
les ont traversées. Les aurores australes laissent-elles des traces
pendant le jour : ces traces se manifestent-elles par une certaine
disposition linéaire de nuages, (*cumulito-stratus* du journal de M. le
Capitaine Fitz-Roy,) également espacés ? Ces rangées de petits
nuages ou *bandes polaires* m'ont paru le plus souvent dirigées dans
le méridien magnétique, p. e. sur le plateau de Mexico, quelquefois,
surtout dans le nord de l'Asie, je les ai vues tourner progressivement
pendant des nuits très-calmes du N. par l'E. N. E. à l'Est. Ces
apparences ne seroient-elles que des effets de perspective, des con-
vergences de stries parallèles, causées par des vents supérieurs ?—
Cette explication me paroît douteuse.

V. Zoologie.

Les mémorables travaux de mon ami et compagnon de voyage, M. Ehrenberg, et les rapports importans de ces travaux, soit avec la connoissance intime de l'organisation d'animaux que l'on croyoit jadis d'une structure infiniment simple, soit avec la phosphorescence de l'océan, et les grandes questions de la Géologie moderne, invitent les naturalistes voyageurs à diriger leurs recherches sur les points suivans :

Recueillir de l'eau de mer partout où l'on aperçoit à la surface des changemens de couleur et de densité, en forme de pellicules, de stries et de taches, huileuses. Dans ces parages il y a abondance d'animaux microscopiques, et comme il est prouvé par l'expérience que ces petits êtres, même les infusoires pélagiques, peuvent, soit à cause de leurs carapaces siliceuses, soit à cause de la consistance de leurs membranes ou tissus organiques, être examinés sous le microscope, après avoir été conservés pendant plusieurs années, on tâchera, j'espère, de les recueillir de deux manières. Là où l'on voit les stries de différentes couleurs, l'on enlèvera une portion de ces stries, en enfonçant dans l'eau de mer des lames très-minces de mica, ou du papier bien fort. Ces lames de mica, ou ces feuilles de papier seront soulevées horizontalement ; on les sechera et les conservera dans un livre, les animaux restant attachés aux mêmes lames de mica ou feuilles de papier, au moyen desquelles on les a recueillis. Dans les parages où l'eau de la mer paroît entièrement pure et presque incolore, elle renferme des acalèphes, des crustacées, et des infusoires microscopiques. Il s'agit seulement de pouvoir examiner ces eaux dans un état pour ainsi dire concentré, d'enfermer les êtres vivans dans un moindre volume du fluide. À cet effet, M. Ehrenberg a l'habitude de faire puiser de l'eau à la surface de la mer dans un seau, et de la faire filtrer ou faire passer à travers un linge très fin, de manière que chaque fois on sépare la portion concentrée qui n'a pas encore passé entièrement à travers le filtre. Ces portions concentrées (plus riches en animaux invisibles à l'œil nu) sont conservées dans de petits flacons de 2 ou 3 pouces de haut. On laisse quelques bulles d'air entre le bouchon et l'eau. Si pendant l'opération de la filtration, on découvre quelques acalèphes visioles à l'œil nu, il faut les séparer et les placer dans l'esprit de vin, afin que ces petites masses gélatineuses n'altèrent pas l'eau de mer concentrée.

Comme ces opérations sont extrêmement faciles, il est à désirer que pendant toute l'expédition, par différens degrés de latitude et de longitude, on recueille de l'eau de mer surtout là où les algues marines abondent. Par les moyens qu'on vient de proposer, on parviendroit à étendre d'une manière inattendue la connaissance de la nature intime des petites organisations et de leur distribution géographique sur le globe. Il ne faut pas oublier que les estomacs remplis de carmin et d'indigo dans tous les Polygastres, que les yeux dans les Rotifères et l'*Eudorina elegans*, et les dents des Hydatines, se conservent pendant de longues années, lorsque ces êtres microscopiques sont préparés entre des lames de mica d'après la méthode de M. Ehrenberg.

Recueillir les animaux qui causent la phosphorescence de l'océan, phosphorescence dans laquelle le *Mammaria scintillans* semble jouer le rôle principal, avec d'autres acalèphes et des infusoires pélagiques (especes de Peridinium, de Synchæta et de Prorocentrum). Observer si la phosphorescence n'est pas plus générale et plus fréquente par un ciel couvert et d'apparence orageuse : examiner si pendant la phosphorescence générale de l'Océan *l'Æquorea forsyocliana, A. phosphorifera*, le *Pelagia cyanella, P. noctiluca* et *P. panopyra*, luisent par scintillation c. a. d. non d'une manière continue, mais en donnant des étincelles par la décharge spontanée de certains organes électriques cellulaires ; conserver ces acalèphes et les béroés phosphoriques dans l'esprit de vin ; examiner si certaines espèces de poissons, *Chimæra arctica, Clupea erythræa, Coryphæna hippuris* et *Scomber pelamys*, sont phosphorescentes par elles-mêmes, ou si ce n'est pas plutôt par l'adhérence d'infusoires phosphorescens.

Recueillir partout celles des substances minérales qui selon les découvertes de M. Ehrenberg, sont composées d'infusoires fossiles comme le tripoli, les schistes à polir, les semi-opales, les minérais de fer limoneux riches en *Galionella ferruginea*, les dépôts colorés des sources salées ou ferrugineuses, les craies, les silex pyromaques, les marnes alternant avec la craie, les dépôts siliceux, les terres que mangent quelques peuples, par goût ou par besoin. Quoique les infusoires à carapaces siliceuses, plus indifférens aux variations des latitudes et des climats, ayent manifesté généralement plus d'aptitude à résister aux grands cataclysmes géologiques, plusieurs des bryozoa calcaires ou polythalames de la craie existent cependant aussi vivans dans la mer actuelle.   M. Ehrenberg en a récemment trouvé de vivans dans la mer Baltique, identiques avec des polythalames enfouies dans les craies et leurs marnes.   Cette circonstance d'identité donne, à cause de l'âge des formations craieuses, un vif intérêt géologique à ce genre d'investigations.

Recueillir et conserver avec soin, à cause des petites organisations qu'ils renferment, les sables des dunes, les sables de toutes les côtes que l'on visite, les sables rejetés par les hautes marées, les sables qui s'attachent à la sonde et à l'ancre des vaisseaux ; recueillir des échantillons des terres qui composent les marais et des endroits inondés et desséchés.   Les plus petites quantités suffisent, en marquant bien exactement les localités où elles ont été receuillies.

VI. Botanique.

Plantes marines qui vivent en société.

Il reste des doutes, si dans certains parages (comme au banc d'algues anciennement connu près des Iles Azores) le *Fucus natans* (*Sargassum vulgare* et *S. bacciferum*, Agardh) continue à végéter sans racines, en flottant à la surface de l'Océan au gré des vents et des courans, ou si le Fucus, récemment arraché à des rochers dont on suppose l'existence et la proximité, ne peut conserver son état de fraîcheur que pendant un très court espace de tems. Les ingénieuses considérations de M. Charles Darwin (Journal, pp. 303—305), ont répandu un nouvel intérêt sur ces "great aquatic forests." L'analogie des Vaucheries et du *Polysperma glomerata*, la facilité même avec laquelle, dans l'eau douce, des plantes phanérogames (l'*Aldrovanda vesiculosa*, et des branches du *Najas major*) continuent à végéter, lorsqu'elles nagent dépourvues de racines, ont fait croire à un voyageur d'une instruction très-variée, M. Meyen, que le *Fucus natans* peut pousser des feuilles (frondes), sans racines et sans adhérence au fond, mais que dans ce cas, le *Fucus natans* flottant ne porte jamais de fruits. Recueillir les échantillons de Fucus qui se sont développés en forme arrondie, les branches s'étendant comme par rayons. Mesurer la température de l'eau la plus froide dans laquelle végètent ces plantes sociales.

(Signé)   ALEXANDRE DE HUMBOLDT.

Berlin, le 26 Octobre, 1839.

Letter from Professor A. Erman to Major Sabine, R.A., F.R.S.

MONSIEUR,   A' Berlin, le 12 Nov. 1839.

J'ai eu le plaisir de vous exprimer à Berlin mon vif intérêt pour l'expédition magnétique, dont votre rapport sur l'intensité totale (*Seventh Report of the British Association for the Advancement of Science*) a fait concevoir le plan, et que le gouvernement Anglais a mis en œuvre avec une munificence entièrement digne du sujèt. Vous savez combien je félicite les voyageurs qui continueront jusqu'aux plus hautes latitudes Australes, les observations que je n'ai poussées que peu au delà du parallèle du Cap Horn, et qui vont tout autant préciser la forme et la position des lignes magnétiques de cet hémisphère, que nous avons pu le faire, M. Hansteen et moi, pour celles de l'Asie du Nord où tout conspiroit à favoriser notre entreprise. Aussi est ce avec beaucoup de reconnoissance que j'accepte l'entremise que vous avez bien voulu m'offrir, pour signaler aux membres de cette grande expédition, quelques résultats et quelques sujèts de recherche, que notre voyage pour un but analogue me porte à recommander à nos successeurs. Il est vrai que la belle instruction dont la Société Royale a muni ses voyageurs, leur indique très complètement les moyens d'obtenir, tant sur mer que lors des mouillages aux côtes et aux glaces polaires, une série continue de déterminations des trois élémens magnétiques. Elle est si riche en détails importans que, dans l'intérêt de la science, on ne sauroit rien desirer au-delà du stricte accomplissement de ce plan de voyage. Cependant pour toujours soutenir l'attention et le zèle dans un travail uniforme d'aussi longue durée, et pour les faire redoubler à point nommé, dans les endroits où les observations augmentent d'importance, il n'y a je crois rien de plus efficace, qu'une comparaison suivie des résultats de l'observation, d'une part avec ceux de la théorie qu'il s'agit de perfectionner, et de l'autre avec les évaluations purement empiriques de ses prédécesseurs. L'expedition antarctique doit jouir de cet avantage pour ses mesures d'intensité totale, en se servant de la carte isodynamique construite d'après la théorie de M. Gauss, et de celle que vous avez directement établie sur les résultats des voyageurs*. J'ai destiné aux mêmes fins la carte ci jointe, Pl. III., représentant *les lignes d'égale déclinaison pour une époque entre 1827 et 1830*. Je les ai obtenues par une interpolation graphique, et devant fournir des isogones indépendantes de toute vue de théorie. J'ai noté sur la carte même les résultats numériques qu'elle représente, et il ne me reste ici qu'à mentionner les voyageurs qui les ont fournis, la direction des routes qu'ils ont suivies, et l'époque de leurs observations.

I. *L'Europe et l'Asie septentrionales.*

MM. *Hansteen* et *Due*, de *Christiania* à *Irkuzk* et à l'embouchure du *Jenisei*, en 1828 et 29.

Erman, de *Berlin* aux bouches de *l'Obi*, par *Irkuzk* et *Ochozk* au *Kamtschatka*, en 1828 et 29.

II. *Le Grand Océan.*

Le Capit. *Lütke* (sur la Corvette le *Siniavine*), du *Cap Horn*, par *Valparaiso*, les iles de *Sitka* et d'*Ounalaska*, à *Petropawlowsk*, en 1827.

Idem (idem) de *Petropawlowsk* à *Manilla*, en 1828.

Erman (la Corvette le *Krotkoi*), de *Petropawlowsk*, par *Sitka*, *San Francisco*, et *Otaheite*, au *Cap Horn*, en 1829 et 30.

III. *L'Atlantique.*

Le Capit. *Lütke* (le *Siniavine*) de l'ile de *Teneriffe*, par *Rio Janeiro*, au *Cap Horn*, en Décembre 1826, et 1827.

Idem (idem) du *Cap de Bonne Espérance*, par les iles de *St. Helène* et de *Fayal*, au *Canal Anglais*, en 1829.

Erman (le *Krotkoi*), du *Cap Horn*, par *Rio Janeiro*, à *Portsmouth*, en 1830.

IV. *La mer des Indes.*

Le Capit. *Hagemeister*, (la corvette le *Krotkoi*), du *Cap de Bonne Espérance*, à *Port Jackson*, en 1828.

Lütke (le *Siniavine*), de *Manilla*, au *Cap de Bonne Espérance*, en 1829.

Je n'ai du ajouter à ces résultats presque contemporains (Dec. 1826 à Oct. 1830) qu'une dixaine d'observations antérieures, toutes faites dans la mer glaciale du Nord, et nommèment par le Capitaine *Wrangel* dans la partie orientale de cette mer (68° à 70° lat., 162° à 182° à l'Est. de Green.) en 1823, et par

* Pls. I. and II.

Le Capitaine *Lütke* dans sa partie occidentale (70° à 77° lat., 27° à 52° à l'Est de Green.) en 1821.

Si l'on compare maintenant dans leur ensemble ce tracé immédiatement calqué sur les observations, et la carte que la théorie de M. *Gauss* a fournie pour la même époque, Pl. IV., on sera frappé de leur accord éminemment satisfaisant, tant pour les formes que pour les places qu'elles assignent à la plûpart des isogones. On envisagera toutefois, comme prévues d'avance, des courbures plus accidentées et moins arrondies dans les isogones empiriques : résultats nécessaires tant d'une interpolation imparfaite d'observations affectées d'erreurs, que d'influences locales, telles que la différente constitution géologique des pays et leurs accidens de climat ; car la théorie que son illustre auteur ne présente que comme une ébauche, ne saurait déja reproduire ces effèts de causes secondaires. Mais, indépendamment de ces écarts accidentels et locaux, une comparaison suivie des deux cartes fait ressortir entre elles quelques différences plus décidément prononcées, portant sur de grandes portions d'isogones bien établies par l'observation. Je me permèts de les signaler ci-après à l'attention de vos voyageurs.

§ 1. Entre 0° et 150° E.

1. *Les sommèts concaves des isogones negatives (orientales) que la carte empirique place vers 77° E., y atteignent de moindres latitudes que d'après la théorie.*

Nommément :

	Sur la carte empirique.	Sur la carte de M. Gauss.
L'isogone de − 15° descend jusqu'à	65° lat.	78° lat.
„ − 10° „	58° 5	64°

2. *Le système de déclinaison positive ou occidentale, qui a son centre d'après l'interpolation graphique vers 130° E., et d'après M. Gauss àpeine 0°.3 à l'ouest de ce même méridien, s'écarte de la théorie par la valeur des lignes qui le composent, et cette différence est l'inverse de la précédente.*

Les sommèts convexes de ces lignes sont,

	Sur la carte empirique.	Sur la carte de M. Gauss.
Pour la courbe de 0° à	68°.5 lat.	61°.7 lat.
„ „ + 2°	65°	54°
„ „ + 6° vers	61°	n'existe pas,

le centre du système situé en 45° lat. ne devant avoir que + 2° 30′ déclin.

On résumera ces deux circonstances, en observant qu'un voyage depuis 65° lat. et 77° E. long. jusqu'en 61° lat. et 130° E. long. offre en réalité un plus fort changement de déclinaison que suivant la théorie. En effèt le changement observé serait de 21° (depuis − 15° jusqu'à + 6°) où la théorie ne demande que 10° (depuis − 10° jusqu'à 0°).

3. *La différence des deux cartes relative à la ligne sans déclinaison entre les dits méridiens n'est au fond qu'une suite de ces deux circonstances (Nos. 1 et 2).* La branche occidentale de cette courbe,

sur laquelle la théorie et l'observation sont presque d'accord, et que cette dernière fait passer par 50° lat. et 48° E. long., se distingue sur les deux cartes par son prolongement vers le Sud et le Sud Est. Elle a son sommet concave sur la carte empirique en −1° lat. et sur la carte de M. Gauss vers −10°· 2 lat. (les latitudes australes étant pris négatives), et passé ce terme, d'après l'observation directe, la courbe se relève vers le Nord Est et le Nord, embrasse le système Asiatique de déclinaison occidentale, pour ne se replier qu'après, par la mer d'Ochozk, le Grand Océan, et la mer des Indes, sur la nouvelle Hollande. La théorie lui assigne au contraire, d'abord après le sommet concave, un rebroussement vers le Sud (en 105° E.), qui la porte directement sur la nouvelle Hollande ; aussi voit on sur la carte de M. *Gauss*, le susdit système de déclinaison occidentale, entouré d'une courbe à zéro fermée et isolée, et dont la branche orientale se trouve plus à l'ouest que ne le demandent les observations pour la partie correspondante de la ligne continue.

En effet ces parties correspondantes de la courbe à zéro coupent :

Sur la carte empirique.	Sur la carte M. Gauss.
Le 60° lat. sous 150° E.,	sous 140° E.
50° „ 151°·3 E.	" 147°·8 E.

Mais je suis loin d'attribuer une spécialité d'intérêt à l'*isogone de zéro* ;—la différence de deux branches isolées, à une courbe continue, que nous venons de lui trouver sur les deux cartes, ne me parait au contraire ni plus ni moins grave, que si elle portait sur quelque autre courbe de ce genre. Je crois plutot que pour voir cet écart dans son vrai jour, il faudra observer que dans le systéme en question, la valeur limite entre des courbes isolées et des courbes continues est, *suivant la théorie* de − 1° 14' *déclin. orientale*, tandis que *l'observation parait l'élever* à une *déclin. occidentale* de + 1°, ou environ, car pour dériver de données numériques la *valeur précise* de cette *limite*, il ne suffit ni d'une interpolation graphique ni d'aucun moyen différent d'une théorie complete. J'observe en outre, et pour me prémunir contre plus de responsabilité que je ne dois avoir sur ce point, que la dite partie de ma carte repose uniquement sur les observations suivantes de M. *Lütke*.

Longit.	Latitude.	Déclinaisons d'après :		L−T.
		M. Lütke.	La théorie.	
		L.	T.	
135° 34'	+ 14° 35'	+0° 10'	− 1°·25	+ 1°·4
134 38	+ 15 34	+ 0 4	− 1	+ 1 ·1
134 04	+ 16 4	+ 1 2	0	+ 1 ·0
122 33	+ 19 54	+ 2 20	+ 0 ·2	+ 2 ·1
117 53	+ 13 41	+ 0 33	− 0 ·8	+ 1 ·3
115 21	+ 13 4	+ 0 23	− 0 ·8	+ 1 ·2
113 03	+ 12 41	+ 0 33	− 1 ·4	+ 2 ·0
105 04	− 8 39	+ 1 26	− 0 ·4	+ 1 ·8
105 32	− 9 46	+ 1 0	− 0 ·2	+ 1 ·2

Malgré leur grande influence sur la forme de la courbe à zéro, ces différences entre la théorie et l'observation sont donc beaucoup plus foibles que celles observées dans les contrées précitées (Nos. 1 et 2) et qui s'élevaient respectivement à — 5° et à + 6°.

Les parties australes des deux cartes situées entre les dits méridiens de 0° à 150° E, s'accordent très bien entre elles.

§ 2. Depuis 150° jusqu'à 360° E.

Il en est de même dans l'hemisphère boréal, depuis 162° jusqu'à 262° E., pour les isogones de —30°, à —15°; mais passé ce terme les courbes théoriques de —12°, de —10°, etc. portent les déclinaisons orientales qu'elles expriment jusqu'à de moindres latitudes boréales que ne l'indique l'observation. Ainsi

	Sur la carte empirique.	La carte de M. Gauss.
L'isogone de — 12° descend jusqu'à	33°·5 lat.	23° lat.
„ „ 6° „ „	28° ·5	17°

C'est cette circonstance, et une toute pareille pour les isogones de même nom dans l'hemisphère austral, qui produisent

4. *Une diversité des deux cartes relativement au système fermé de déclinaison orientale dans le Grand-Océan.*

Les courbes de — 10°, — 9°, et — 8° sont les parties de ce système que l'observation directe a le mieux reconnues, et nous trouvons à *chacune d'elles* plus d'étendue dans le sens du méridien que ne l'adopte la théorie. Ainsi d'après

		La carte empirique.	La carte de M. Gauss.
L'isog. de — 10° va	{ depuis + 27°·8 lat.	+ 17° lat.
	{ jusqu'à — 49°·5	— 39
„ — 9° „	{ depuis + 25	+ 12°·5
	{ jusqu'à — 47	— 36
„ — 8° „	{ depuis + 23	+ 7°·5
	{ jusqu'à — 44°·5	— 34°

Leurs diamètres dans le sens du méridien sont donc respectivement :

d'après *l'observation directe* de 77°·3, 72° et 67°·5, et d'après *l'interpolation théoretique* de 56°, 43°·5 et 41°·5.

Les observations nous apprennent en outre sur les isogones de ce système, que celle de —10° passe bien décidément d'un pole nord à un pole sud, et qu'au contraire la courbe de —8° est *isolée et rentrante.* L'isogone de —9° participe tellement aux propriétés de ces deux espèces de courbes, que, parmi celles que représente ma carte, elle doit être la plus voisine de la valeur limite. La théorie s'y accorde très bien en indiquant —8° 46'·5 pour cette même limite. L'accord des deux cartes est moins parfait sur la position du centre de ce système et sur la déclinaison qui y règne, car la forme des courbes empiriques de—10° à—7° engagerait a le présumer situé

vers 231°·8 E.
—12° lat.

tandis que l'interpolation théorique le porte en
219°·8 E.
—14°·5 lat.
aussi la théorie attribue à ce point une *déclinaison minimum* de
—5°15',mais nous avons très souvent observé sur le Krotkoi,demême
que Mr. Lütke sur la route plus orientale du Siniavin, des déclinaisons entre—5° et—4° et mêmes quelques unes de—3°50'à—3°40'.
Nous étions cependant encore très sensiblement eloignés du centre
des courbes.

5. *Dans l'hemisphère austral entre les meridiens de* 192° E. *et*
262° E. *les isogones de*—12° *et de*—15°, *d'après la théorie ne s'ap-*
procheraient du pole austral que jusqu'aux parallèles de —38°·8 *et de*
—49°, *tandis que les observations paraissent les y étendre jusqu'en*
—52°·7 *et* — 58°.

Mais je termine cette comparaison, en vous priant, Monsieur,
d'accorder encore votre attention à l'harmonie très parfaite des deux
cartes relativement au système de déclinaison occidentale qui re-
couvre l'Atlantique et l'Europe, lequel, vu la grande fréquence des
observations dans ces parages, est un des plus solidement établis par
l'expérience directe. La théorie porte la *valeur limite pour ce sy-*
stème à+22° 13', et les observations démontrent, d'abord, que cette
même valeur est comprise entre +20° et +25°; et de plus, qu'elle
est beaucoup plus rapprochée de la moyenne arithmétique de ces
deux nombres, que d'aucun d'eux.

Je passe à quelques autres sujets de recherche que je me permets
de résumer en de simples questions :

Aurores Polaires. Y *a-t-il dans les hautes latitudes antarctiques*
quelque indication d'une duplicité d'Aurores Polaires ? Les habitans
de *Bérésow* sur l'Obi (63° 56' N. lat.) en distinguent en effèt de
deux espèces : de plus foibles ayant leurs centres à l'Ouest; et de
plus brillantes qui se forment à l' Est du meridien. Les données que
j'ai pu recueillir sur les azimuts où se formeraient ces deux phénomènes m'ont fait présumer qu'ils surgissent respectivement de l'un
ou de l'autre des deux foyers magnétiques de l'hemisphère boréal.

Phosphorescence de la mer. *Existe-t-il un minimum de tempé-*
rature qui empècheroit d'avoir lieu le développement de lumière opéré
par des Méduses, des Scolopendres, et surtout par des Crustacés mi-
croscopiques vaguement qualifiés de Zoophytes infusoires?
J'ai observé des phases très brillantes de ce phénomène sur la
mer d'Ochozk dans les nuits du

3 *Aout* par +39°·2 F. température de la mer.
5 *Aout* „ +41 ·0 „
6 *Aout* „ +41 ·2 „
7 *Aout* „ +46 ·6 „

mais il y eut cessation parfaite la nuit du 4 *Aout* où la température
de la mer baissa jusqu' à +37°·4 F.

Un phénomène lumineux, différent d'apparence et d'origine, s'observe sur la même mèr d'*Ochozk* à l'approche de la saison froide, et
y est connu sous le nom de *Spolochi.* Ce sont des bandes lumineuses,

qui paraissent douées d'un mouvement propre, et qui se repandent en jets rayonnans, depuis un centre commun à plusieurs d'entr'elles et également situé à la surface de la mer. On ne saurait les confondre avec la lumière due aux Mollusques, laquelle ne forme jamais des bandes, mais des points distinctement isolés, et brillans de préférence dans le sillage du vaisseau, dans les brisans, et sur l'écume des lames et des vagues. Les bandes en question ressemblent au contraire à de la lumière électrique qui se répandrait à la surface d'un conducteur imparfait. *Y a-t-il des phénomènes analogues dans l'hemisphère austral, et quelles circonstances paroissent les provoquer ?*

Météorologie.

A égalité de latitude, la moyenne hauteur du baromètre m'a paru moindre sur le grand Océan que sur la mer Atlantique : *la même différence s'observe-t-elle encore sur les prolongemens des méridiens en question jusqu'à de hautes latitudes Antarctiques ?*

Sur le grand Océan, entre le 50° et 60° de latitude nord, c'est bien décidément le *vent d'Ouest* qui augmente la pression atmosphérique au dessus de la valeur moyenne. Cet effet du *vent d'Ouest* est le contraire de ce que l'on observe en Europe, et il me parait fort intéressant de recueillir sur ce point des données correspondantes dans l'hémisphère austral.

J'ai vu avec beaucoup de plaisir que la Société Royale dirige l'attention de ses voyageurs sur la différence de la colonne barométrique aux limites polaires et aux limites équatoriales des zones alizées. Voici les résultats que j'ai obtenus à cet égard de mes propres observations. (*Poggendorf, An. der Physik für* 1831.)

Mois.	Longit.	Alizé N.E. Diff. des haut barom.	Mois.	Longit.	Alizé S.E. Diff. des haut barom.
Mai et Juin..	167°	3$^{\prime\prime\prime}$·154	Mai	179°	2$^{\prime\prime\prime}$·245
Janvier	233	0 ·929	Jan. et Fev.	222	2 ·714
Juil. et Aout..	327	3 ·016	Juin et Juil.	324	2 ·453
Novembre ..	342	2 ·668	Decembre..	333	1 ·492

Les différences sont exprimées en *lignes* du *pied de Paris*, et se rapportent aux colonnes barométriques observées à la limite polaire et à la limite équatoriale de la zone alizée.

Essuie-t-on jamais des orages sur mer quand on est à la fois à une grande distance de toute côte, et loin des limites des alizés ? L'expérience d'une seule année ne m'en a fourni aucun exemple.

Etoiles filantes.

Si les voyageurs antarctiques ont le loisir d'observer le retour périodique des étoiles filantes du 10 Août ou du 13 Nov., il seroit fort à desirer qu'ils fissent attention à la direction apparente de leur mouvement, et que nommément ils dessinassent sur une carte céleste leurs trajectoires apparentes, pour examiner après, si *leurs prolongemens se coupent en un même point du ciel.* Les étoiles tombantes de 1839, Août 10, convergeaient toutes vers le point du ciel :

Ascens. droite 222°·4
Declinaison .. 51°·2 Australe.

L'instruction de la Société Royale ayant dirigé l'attention des voyageurs sur la *Chionis Alba,* je me permets de leur communiquer que nous avons pris dans deux jours consécutifs 5 ou 6 de ces oiseaux, en nous trouvant à la hauteur des *iles Falklands,* et à une distance de 48 à 60 milles marins de leur extrémité orientale. Il est vrai que ce fut par un vent *d'ouest assez frais,* mais on ne saurait cependant décider sans recherche ultérieure, si ces oiseaux intéressans ne sont pas engagés par quelque autre cause à s'éloigner des côtes qu'ils habitent. Les *Chionis* nous ont paru si propres à la domesticité que l'on pourrait sans doute les conserver vivantes jusqu'au retour en Europe, et peut être même en faire propager l'espèce. Il est fort probable qu'ils se nourrissent de préférence de grains ou d'autres semences dures, car nous leur avons constamment trouvé dans l'estomac du sable et de petits cailloux, que nous croyions destinés à faciliter la trituration et la digestion de pareilles substances.

Je termine ces remarques détachées en me recommandant, Monsieur, à l'indulgence que vous daignates si souvent témoigner à

Votre tres devoué serviteur,

M. le Major Sabine, R.A.   A. ERMAN.

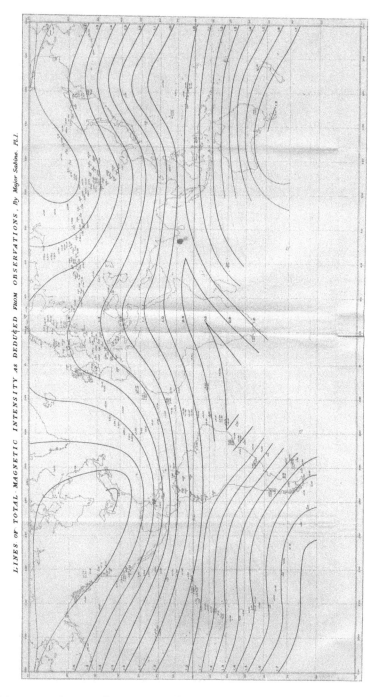

LINES OF TOTAL·MAGNETIC INTENSITY AS DEDUCED FROM OBSERVATIONS, By Major Sabine, F.L.I.

The material originally positioned here is too large for reproduction in this reissue. A PDF can be downloaded from the web address given on page iv of this book, by clicking on 'Resources Available'.

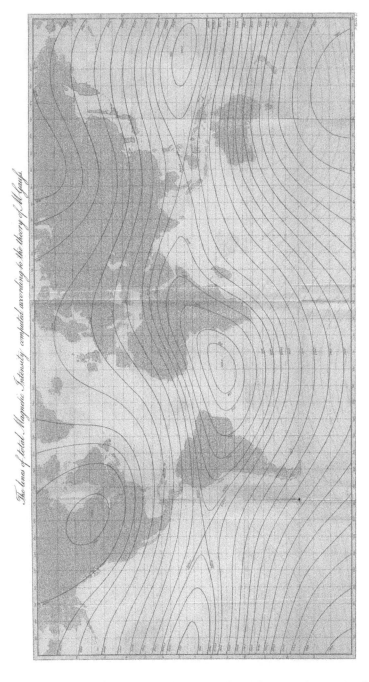

The lines of total Magnetic Intensity computed according to the theory of M.Gauss.

The material originally positioned here is too large for reproduction in this reissue. A PDF can be downloaded from the web address given on page iv of this book, by clicking on 'Resources Available'.

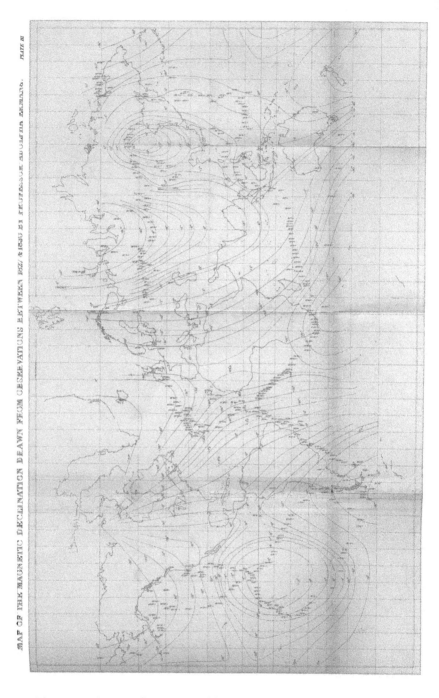

PLATE IV

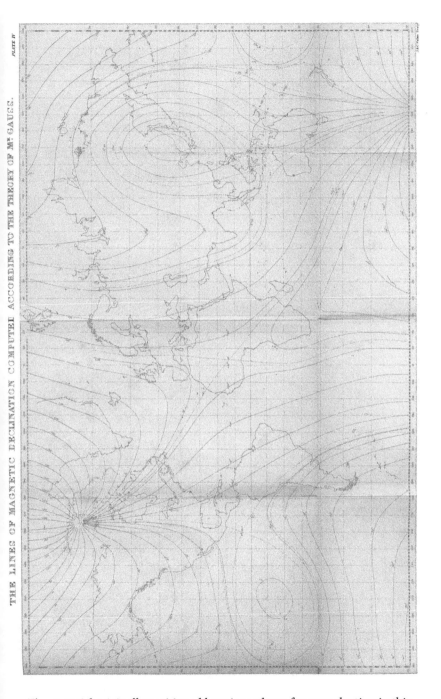

The material originally positioned here is too large for reproduction in this reissue. A PDF can be downloaded from the web address given on page iv of this book, by clicking on 'Resources Available'.